The KiSS System

Keep. It. Simple. Stupid.

Stress-Free Marketing Strategies to Boost Your Local Business on a Budget!

CONNIE S. GORRELL

Printed and released in the U.S.A.
General editing: Cori Collins

If unable to purchase this book from your local bookseller, you may order directly fromwww.amazon.com or via the publisher's website.

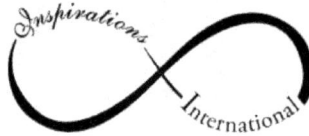

Creative Works to Inspire the World

www.inspirations.international

ISBN: 978-0-9982651-4-8
ISBN-10: 0-9982651-4-4
Library of Congress Control Number: 2018902167

DEDICATION

I dedicate this book to small business owners everywhere: To those overcoming every obstacle to start a business, the mom & pop shops, to struggling parents with an entrepreneurial spirit, and to those with a great idea and the passion to see it through. You deserve to be in the limelight. This book is for you!

The KiSS System

Keep. It. Simple. Stupid.

The KISS Principle Defined

KISS is an acronym attributed to aeronautical engineer Kelly Johnson. It is a design principle that stands for **"Keep It Simple, Stupid."** It was most noted by the United States Navy in 1960. The KISS principle states, in essence, that all systems work best when kept **simple** rather than made complicated.

And so it shall be with your stress-free marketing strategies!

TABLE OF CONTENTS

Introduction

WHY DIDN'T I THINK OF THAT!?

Have you honed the single most profitable skill needed to run a successful business? It's not keeping the shelves stocked. It isn't managing employees. It's not even having a good product.

No. The most important skill you need to have mastered is the art of *marketing* your business. And, make no mistake, it is vital to your success. Why? Because the only time you can bring money into your business is when you actually sell something, right? It could be tangible products or standard services. You can't stock the shelves or hang your shingle unless you have the cash flow to buy the supplies to put on the shelves and keep your business open and operational.

You can't pay your employees, or yourself for that matter, unless you have money coming in from selling your unique products or services. A great product could just as well be a piece of junk in a trunk if no one knows it exists. I am here to see that does not happen to you.

This is why you need to learn how effective and targeted marketing strategies play a key role in your local business success; but we will take it beyond that. We will devise your own marketing strategies in simple ways, and on a budget you can easily swing. You will creatively communicate to your clients or the public that you have a unique product, that you offer a good consumer experience, and that they should repeatedly buy from you rather than from your competitors. That is what this book is about.

Marketing could be the most misunderstood skill on the planet. That's why it is an art—something to be honed, tested and perfected.

1

Poor marketing is one reason why over sixty-five percent of new businesses close their doors within two years, and more than eighty-five percent of businesses don't make it eight years before going belly-up. How unfortunate; and mostly avoidable.

There is a good chance that most of your competitors do not understand how to effectively market their business in order to achieve the results they seek. They are still stuck, trying to think outside the box. I do not want you to think outside the box—I want you to think like there *is no box*. By knowing a few simple secrets, you will be at a great advantage over the competition. Isn't that what it's all about in business? By learning the techniques and tools shared in this book, you will be able to beat your competitors at the starting gate.

I started, or should I say 'stumbled' into, my first business in the mid-nineties. I had been a registered nurse educator with a background in critical care. Through a series of coincidences, I found myself at the helm of a thriving business that offered continuing education credits to healthcare professionals. I knew nothing about marketing my company, other than the 'just get out there and do it' philosophy. I learned early that I wasn't dreaming large enough. I suppose I was afraid to dream big and risk getting hurt. But I learned that the world was waiting for what I had to offer—I just had to do the work to get it out there. I wanted to make my company stand out in the crowd, so I started concocting unique campaigns that really took off. At one point I convinced our state department of health to invest in my women's programs and travel the state with me, along with a few physician speakers in tow.

To make a long story short, we ended up doing conferences from coast to coast across America and into Mexico. The demand for our services expanded into the community-at-large in addition to the healthcare professionals. We did network television and radio interviews as well as global podcasts. We hosted famous international celebrities, too! Who knew!? I don't share this with you to brag. I share this to make a point: All things are possible. Be creative. Be unique. Your community is waiting for what you have to offer, but they have to know you are there.

I originally wrote *The Art of Local Advertising* in the fall of 2011. The marketing landscape has changed in leaps and bounds since then. It seems somewhat daunting, but it is also exciting. There are more opportunities than ever to market your business in new and innovative ways but learning to navigate the changes may be a challenge for some. I've heard it before: *I'm a business person, not a marketer! I don't know where to start. What am I supposed to do*?

I want you to know this: I hear you. It is because of the dynamics behind this very question that I decided to write a new and updated book to offer you advantages with newly created tools. There is enough stress in this world to go around. This book, *The KISS System: Stress-Free Marketing Strategies to Boost Your Local Business on a Budget*, is filled with unique and creative secrets that you can implement quickly to set your business apart from your competitors, and on a limited budget, if not free! I will take the anxiety out of it for you. Relax. Remember this: In the land of the blind, the person with one good eye is king. Loyalty equates to royalty when it comes to your customers. The trick is letting *them* know that. This book will show you how and it will leave your competitors scratching their heads saying, "Why didn't *I* think of that?"

You are about to learn some straightforward, proven, powerful (and profitable!) marketing strategies that you can start using today to become business royalty in your own local marketplace, and in pretty short order, too! You have, right now in your hands, information that could change your life—and your business— forever. Use it wisely and profit. Are you ready? Let's get started.

Here's to your business, your labor of love, your work of art—and to your success!

Connie

4

Chapter One

MAKE NO MISTAKE

Can you name the Big Three when it comes to costly mistakes that almost all small businesses make at some point, if not continuously? If you can't, you are certainly not alone. Most entrepreneurs and business managers simply have never considered the fact that by making three small tweaks to their current business plan, they can increase sales by up to twenty percent within the next one hundred days. It's absolutely true.

I know that some of these ideas will surprise you. In fact, I hope they do. Why? Because my job is to help you take a fresh look at your own business and evaluate the areas that can be improved *right now* in order to create more sales geared to improve your bottom line immediately. What I love about the ideas and strategies you are going to see here is that they are simple—the kind that make you say, "*Why didn't I think of that*!?" You are going to apply my KISS System (Keep It Simple Stupid) throughout this book. Isn't it time you learned how to create your own successful and unique marketing strategies that make you stand out in today's super competitive marketplace? The answer is a resounding yes!

By the way, I am not calling you stupid. Contraire. I think you've made a very wise decision for the longevity of your business by taking these steps toward your success. Just keep your marketing strategies stupidly simple and you will see remarkable results. Remember this: *If it's stupid, but it works, it's not stupid.*

Today's competitive climate presents new challenges and, better yet, exciting opportunities for success. Make haste to take full advantage of them. Your customers await the experience that only *you* can provide.

As you know, customers now have more choices than ever so making savvy marketing and advertising choices can be the difference between consumer excitement about your business or indifference altogether. I don't want you to get lost in market saturation.

First, it is important to know the differences between the terms advertising, *marketing*, and *public relations*. In a nutshell it goes like this:

- **Advertising** is actually paying (usually dearly) for ad space in a newspaper, magazine or other media outlets such as television, internet or radio.

- **Marketing** is the promotion of your business through a variety of campaigns such as community involvement, social media, attending trade shows, sending newsletters or postcards among other promotional activities.

- **Public Relations** targets getting your business, services, event or product mentioned in the media.

Get ready because we are going to pull out all the stops as we go sailing over your competition's head. This is your schooling on how to promote your small business to your loyal clients for free or cheap. Take that which is pertinent to your business and use the techniques within. As with any book you read, there is valuable information mixed with tidbits that may not apply to your situation as much. I have attempted to include wide variables in hopes of capturing relatable information that will help you run your business marketing effectively. My goal is to help you learn how to customize the concepts to your particular business needs.

Be Outstanding in Your Field

Before we dive into the nitty gritty of local marketing, allow me these few words of advice. Here are some great ways to stand out in your local area head and shoulders above the rest. These are simple ideas that will cost you little to no money, and they are highly effective.

- Get involved with your community to get more "face time" with your buying public.

- Collect food or articles of clothing for your local food bank and support charities.

- Sponsor sports teams, a local trash clean-up day or look into planting attractive trees and flowers in public places (but check with local officials first).

- Support local school events and place advertisements in their school programs and newsletters.

These are all effective ways of getting noticed in the local media. Not bad for free or cheap advertising. Is your competition out in the community doing these things? If they are not, then you need to hit the ground running. This is a unique opportunity for you to surge ahead. This is my KISS System at its finest.

What we discuss in this book may be new methods to you, but I urge you to read them with an open mind. Challenging times call for new ideas! You are creating your masterpiece, after all. Marketing your business in a new way can be quite enjoyable and publicly enlightening.

Keep *The KISS System: Stress-Free Marketing Strategies to Boost Your Local Business on a Budget* with you as your personal guide and smile slyly at the marketing strategies you gain (it will make your competition wonder what you're up to—but only *you* will know the answer). But seriously, we are going to discuss and discover highly targeted, extremely individualized and unique ways of situating your business to stand out among the rest.

One merchant I know wrapped a huge red ribbon around the front of the store during their anniversary sale; another put a pig in the window. You could put a bull in your china shop, but it isn't recommended or even necessary. I am going to give you the goods needed to make your company stand out and away from the competition.

My definition of a customer is this:

> One who indirectly pays for your vacations, hobbies and groceries, and awards you the opportunity to improve the quality of life for yourself and your family.

At the beginning of this chapter I mentioned the "Big Three." These are the top three marketing mistakes usually overlooked and vastly misunderstood. This is exactly why it is imperative that we discuss them now. Remember, keep an open mind.

Most common mistakes made by small and local business owners when they create their marketing strategies:

Mistake #1: Going after new customers only

Mistake #2: Not effectively using cross-sells, up-sells or packaged deal techniques

Mistake #3: Not completely understanding the lifetime value of a loyal customer

---

Now let's break down the Big Three individually. If any ideas come to mind as you read on, jot them down in the marketing journal and workbook pages at the end of each chapter so you can revisit them later.

MISTAKE #1:

SOLEY MARKETING TO GAIN NEW CUSTOMERS

That's a mistake? Yes, you read that right. But before you roll your eyes, hear me out. New customers are the *most expensive* people in the world to find, attract into your place of business, acquire, then convert into regular paying customers. My point is: Concentrate on your loyal customers—you know who they are. They are the familiar ones that already patronize your business consistently and appreciate what you have to offer. They are golden.

It is a direct line of wisdom to consider your current clients and regular customer base as your best resource for drumming up new business. Word-of-mouth advertising (whether good or not-so-good) is very effective within any local community. Online reviews have been an absolute game changer when it comes to your customers leaving feedback in regard to your product or services. You can start by setting aside a specific amount of time per week dedicated solely to identifying ways to keep your best clients happy with your services. We will go into this in more detail.

To help drive home the importance of your existing customer base, I will demonstrate a powerful fact.

There are three ways to increase your profit margins.

Let's say young Brantley has set up a lemonade stand on a busy sidewalk. He sells one cup a day to one hundred people and charges ten cents per cup for a total of $10.00 a day in profit, minus expenses. Not a bad day for the young entrepreneur, but if little Brantley figures out a way to get two hundred people to buy a cup of his lemonade per day, he doubles his earnings. That's not the only way he can double his gains.

What if he comes up with an incentive for his existing customers to each purchase two cups of lemonade instead of one? By doing this, he doubles his profits with the same number of customers.

In addition, what if he were to offer something for his customers to purchase that is complementary to the lemonade, such as a cookie? Then, if a certain percentage of his customers also buys a cookie when he sells them lemonade, Brantley just significantly increased his sales.

Again, there are three specific ways to grow your business and increase profits. We discussed numbers one and two, but here are all three:

1. Increase your overall number of customers

2. Offer customers more items to purchase per visit

3. Get regular customers to purchase more items per visit *and* offer incentives to entice them to visit your business more frequently

Of the three, which do you feel is the most profitable? Think about it this way: Say you spend $2,500 a year on a newspaper advertisement and say it brings you one hundred prospective customers.

In essence, you have paid $25 for each person that entered your store who *might* purchase from you. That is a static cost. You paid that $25 per person whether they purchased something from you or not—or even if they bought one of everything in the store. It doesn't matter. You already paid. In addition, you also paid for those consumers that never laid eyes on the ad but happened along into your store anyway.

What if you could increase the average transaction value of each customer by just $10? What would it cost you? Usually nothing but a few minutes of creative thought. You already paid the $25 to get them into the store so you might as well maximize their value.

As in little Brantley's case, he used what is referred to as *cross-selling* on his patrons that purchased a cookie. It is simply a matter of creatively grouping complementary goods and using the right language to get the highest number of people to say yes to purchasing something in addition to what they originally came in to the store to buy in the first place.

Many years ago, McDonald's started something ginormous by asking one simple question, and I bet you know exactly what that is: "Would you like fries with that?" What do you suppose was the extra cost for McDonald's to do this? Maybe two minutes of training for the employee; two seconds for the employee to say it to each customer; two seconds for the customer to say yes. Done deal. Massive impact. The result: An overall jump of about $0.08 in profit *per customer*—and with, as McDonald's likes to say, "Over 99 billion served," that's a brimming bucket full of profit! If you constituted this type of program, you can enjoy your day in the sun!

Go for the Gold

It is said that all is not gold that glitters, but I am going to share two golden nuggets to use as a rule of thumb that can help turn your business into gold if you pay close attention. Hint: They both deal with your *existing valued customer base*. Ready?

> **Golden Nugget #1:**
>
> Spend more of your time and energy finding ways to get customers who have already purchased from you in the past, or your new prospects, to **purchase *more*** from your business each time they visit.

> **Golden Nugget #2:**
>
> Devise creative campaigns, incentives and specials that entice your existing customers to make **more frequent visits**.

Sometimes the last thing you need is more unattached customers. Problems you currently may have in your business usually multiply when you bring new customers into the funnel. Instead, figure out how to get *more* business from the *same* number of your good customers. Besides, word-of-mouth advertising that your regular customers do on your behalf is more than enough to bring in the perfect types of new clientele for your business.

The New Customer vs. Current Customer: Value Check

Take note of some basic important customer criteria required to make your marketing efforts work optimally well for you. Can you check these off your criteria list?

- ✓ Customers must know you exist.

- ✓ Customers must want (and afford) what you are selling.

- ✓ Customers must know, like and trust you.

Obviously, new customers first need to hear about your products or services. They need to know that your business exists and that your consumer experience is second to none. Your marketing and referrals must be optimally on target.

But that's not enough. They must also be in the market for what you offer. Do not attempt to sell ice cream to Eskimos. Keep your finger on the pulse of your industry by watching for fads and buying trends of your demographic. Social media awareness is a must in this realm, but we will go into that in a bit.

And finally, new customers must trust you enough to willingly hand over their hard-earned dollars to receive the value you promise to deliver to them.

Now let's turn to your current customers. They already know you exist and have already demonstrated that they need at least some of what you offer. At one point in their life they trusted you enough to exchange their dollars for the value you promised and delivered to them.

All else being equal, who do you think will be more inclined to say yes to your next offer? A stranger? Or someone who knows you and is likely to be comfortable dealing with you again—someone for whom you previously provided a good service experience?

I think the answer is obvious. Before we go into how to get former customers to increase the frequency of which they purchase from you, let us first deal with increasing the average purchasing size from each customer individually.

> ### *Create Specialized Existing Customer Loyalty Programs*
>
> *Loyalty programs get a jump on the competition. Loyal clients rave to their friends and family about the services you provide and the experience they encounter with you. When they share a positive review, new customers find their way to your doorstep, too. **You wind up with new customers simply by taking special care of your existing ones.***

MISTAKE #2:

NOT EFFECTIVELY USING CROSS~SELLS, UP~SELLS, OR PACKAGED~DEAL SELLING

Cross~Sells:

We discussed *cross-sells* with the McDonald's "Would you like fries with that?" example. So, what could this mean for your business? The first thing you need to do is to design and implement your own unique cross-sells.

There is a fairly simple way to do that. Look at the five to seven most popular selling items in your business. Each one of them should have a cross-sell. For example, in the flooring business (apply the following concepts into your particular business type or category), when people buy carpeting, you could also have an exclusive offer for them to buy a spot removal product along with their new carpeting.

You can even offer a special 'purchase discount' because you don't need as high of margins since you have already paid (in marketing and advertising) to attract these customers to come in the door and purchase from you in the first place.

Give this some thought. Select your five best sellers and find other items that you can offer that complement these main purchases, in the same way as fries ideally complement a cheeseburger. What would be your best cross-selling items?

Simply create a quick script to use and train your employees to use this technique. It could be something as simple as "Would you be interested in receiving a special fifty percent VIP discount on spot remover to complement your beautiful new flooring purchase today?"

Anything is better than nothing. Based on tests, even a weak attempt at a cross-sell works six to twenty-five percent of the time. The point is that cross-sells involve virtually no hard cost or effort at all to implement, so why not do it?

Up-Sells:

The second action is the *up-sell*. This is where you offer your customer a more premium version of what they stand ready to purchase. Let's return to the flooring example.

There are different pads you can put under your carpet. There is the basic or standard pad, often made of several varied materials that are bonded together, thus making it cheaper to sell to the client. Then there is the premiere pad, which is solid, more durable, makes the flooring last longer, but is more expensive.

In this case, when putting together an offer for the customer, you could say something like "Would you like to invest a little bit more to make this carpet last 6 years longer and feel more comfortable under your feet?" Then, you simply explain exactly why buying the upgraded version of the padding is a better option for them.

Think about it this way—if your mark-up is the same for both types of padding, you make more money by selling them the more expensive carpet pad. Example: Let's say you make fifty percent profit on each pad you sell. If a customer needs 100 square yards of the basic pad and that sells for $4.50 per square yard, then you just sold $450 of materials, of which $225 is profit to you.

So, bump them up to the premium pad that sells for $7.50 per square yard. That's $750 in material sold, of which $375 is profit in your pocket.

You achieved an increase of $150 for just a few minutes of sales work. Again, all you have to do is come up with a simple script, and a simple way to demonstrate why the little bit of extra cost involved for the customer is worth the investment in terms of what they are going to get for that little extra bit of cost.

So how can you make this work for you? Go back to your best five to seven popular products and simply ask yourself, "Is there an upgraded or premium version of this that I can offer to my customers?"

The answer is going to be yes: There always is; just be creative and keep it simple. Often, you can create a premium version without hardly any additional hard cost, if you focus on intangibles. Let me give you an example.

Say you own a high-end restaurant. One premium version you can offer to your clients is your special *Immediate Seating VIP Club*. For a small fee each year, you can guarantee that these customers get seated as soon as they enter the restaurant.

In this case, you are selling time and convenience, not a product. That has a lot of value in this day and age. People like upgrades and conveniences, not to mention a VIP experience and will visit more frequently for the experience (and because they paid for it).

Or you could even create a special area for preferred customers; one that has a much more luxurious climate to it, to allow them to enjoy the atmosphere more. Again, you are selling luxury, not a product; another intangible. An experience.

I have heard it said that the happiest people buy *experiences*, not *things*. Think about that. How can you provide an exclusive experience for your loyal customers in your particular setting?

Packaged-Deal Selling:

The final sales technique you should consider using is *packaged selling*. Most people prefer to have someone else make the decision for them, so they don't have any responsibility in the matter.

As in the flooring example, why not create an *Active Lifestyle Package*? This would be for people with young children, maybe pets as well, or for those who have high traffic areas in their homes or businesses.

For this special package, you choose the carpet, padding, vinyl and tile options, and then sell it as a package, instead of each component on its own. This allows you to already *include* the premium versions, or the products that have the highest profit margins and price them accordingly.

Your customers are more likely to say yes, if you do it right, since it makes it easier for them to say yes when the decisions are made for them. This could serve you well as a salon owner or pet groomer, too.

The next logical step is to up-sell them to an even more deluxe package. In this case it could be the *Active & Luxurious Lifestyle Package*.

Going back to our restaurant example, let's design a *Romance Package*. In this case, the customer gets a special table near the fireplace that is more secluded, they get a vase filled with beautiful flowers, perhaps to take home as a keepsake, and they get a *Lover's Dessert* for the lucky couple to share. You are no longer in the restaurant business. Now you are in the romance business—and you can charge a lot more for that!

At the very least, create one package deal that you can offer to a certain portion of your clients. Make it higher priced and more exclusive than normal so that even if only a handful of customers say yes to it each year, you'll have made a pretty good extra bit of profits without doing hardly any more work. Your marketing consultant can be of value to assist you on this as well.

MISTAKE #3:

UNDERESTIMATING THE LIFETIME VALUE OF A LOYAL CUSTOMER

If you knew the potential lifetime value of even one average customer, you would spend far more time making sure existing customers continued to use your services, and far less time trying to get new customers.

Let me give you an example. Let's say Jacquie is a forty-year-old local woman who is on a thrifty food plan to feed her family of three. Say she spends on the average $150 a week at her preferred grocery store. Jacquie is established in her home and community and does not plan on moving any time soon. She has at least thirty more years of good shopping left in her and, so far, has been a loyal customer.

So, doing the math, thirty years is 1,560 weeks. And at a minimal average of $150 per week in groceries at today's prices, that's $234,000 she spends in your store over the next thirty years. This totals over a quarter of a million dollars...and that's just one customer! If you owned that grocery store, don't you think it would be prudent to come up with a strategy to make sure that Jacquie keeps coming back to you? What about Jacquie's kids who marry and live near-by? They would be potentially considered to be lifetime customers, too. You could stand to gain another generation of loyal customers.

Previous studies on customer traffic were recently retested, and their accuracy was reconfirmed. Once again, they reaffirmed which scenarios resulted in customers *not* further patronizing a store or a service provider.

Here is what they learned about customer traffic:

- **9% leave to go to the competition**

Okay, sure, a competitor might come along and offer them a better deal or better service. Perhaps they have a location that is preferable over yours. Though unfortunate, that is part of the game. Nonetheless the instructive thing to recognize is that you only lose nine percent of your customers because of this (though there are methods of reducing this as we have discussed and will continue as we go along). You may gain that nine percent back under the same rule, too.

- **9% leave because they move away**

It is hard to get someone to come back to your store if they move away from the area. It's just the nature of today's mobile society. Some will move because we are, by nature, nomadic creatures, especially these days.

- **14% leave because of a complaint or dissatisfaction with service or product you provide**

This aspect can be worked on a bit, but one thing I have learned in business is you can't please everyone, nor do you want to. Anyway, it is not that big of a deal because there is one aspect that is far, *far* greater that causes your customers to go somewhere else for services that you provide.

This one is greater than all these other factors combined—and it pains me greatly to say...

- **68% percent take their business elsewhere because of perceived apathy of the service provider**

Perceived apathy of the service provider! Excuse me while I go get a cool, damp cloth for my forehead. That one is utterly avoidable. This issue is very critical and is almost exclusively what lead to the sole purpose for the creation of this book.

In other words, your customer felt that you only look at them as someone from whom to get money, and that you don't really care about them after the sale. Notice the word *perceived.* You know the old saying, "What one perceives to be true becomes their truth."

You might very well care a great deal about them, but if you don't show them you care in a way that is unique and isn't something that everyone else already does, then there is no reason for them to remain loyal to you. I can speak personally and tell you that I have taken my loyal business elsewhere on several occasions for this very reason. As a consumer, haven't you?

Sometimes we are simply too busy or we feel too overwhelmed to goosh the goodness and ooze excitement over our clients coming through the door. I get that. But knowledge is power and just being aware of how you could be coming across may help you and your staff remember to brighten your smiles when you address your customers. Make their day brighter, too.

If you don't have a specific customer retention strategy in place, you could be losing two-thirds of your previous customers. When you consider the potential lifetime value of one single customer, that should make you cringe.

So, what is the remedy? First, you need to increase the amount of communication you have with your customers. Design a program that focuses on staying in touch with your loyal patrons. Depending on the business you are in, you could consider methods for personal follow up, either by email, phone, in store specials, hand written letter or in person.

Brand Journalism:

Consider a developing a newsletter, and no, not one of those fancy, corporate looking newsletters of which I am sure you are familiar. Take a more personal approach and allow your business establishment's unique personality shine through.

People do not fall in love with corporations. They fall in love with personalities. The first part of that word is *person*. Open up to them. Let them know who you are and a little bit about what is going on in your business. You should show some character and a bit of humor and style as well as useful information and great deals.

Think of why you are close friends with the friends you have chosen in your life. Try to establish that same type of bond with your customers. There are several strategies I use for this purpose, such as creating a monthly or quarterly newsletter or ezine (electronic newsletter). I call this *brand journalism*. It is one way for a business owner to take control of their public image, or their brand, by publishing news and information about the business on a regular basis. You don't want to buy marketing services; you want to buy more customers—more profits! Keeping on top of your business reputation is key to keeping your customers engaged. A regular newsletter can help with that. Highlight a customer, announce staff news, create an event. Let your customers really get to know you.

There are some good copywriters looking for work that can provide you with affordable content if you don't have the time, desire, or talent to do it yourself. College kids love these types of opportunities. Engage one of them to do the copywriting if it's not your thing. Talk to your customers, too. You might be surprised to learn of their expertise and willingness to contribute articles for your newsletter—especially if they are a local business owner who would join forces with you and share the opportunity and the expense.

Finally, someone who cares about you looks out for your best interest with no ulterior motive in mind. Again, that is where a newsletter could come in handy. Each month, you can create an article giving your customers tips on how to better their life, improve the value they can get from your services, care for the products you sell them, recipes, and other things that can make them feel better about themselves and their situation. Offer them a special promotion or a discount. They will know they are getting all this just because they are a customer of yours!

And *that* is how you make a customer feel valued.

Do you now see why the Big Three misconceptions are really big mistakes? Realize that they are only mistakes if you fail to heed them. But you are not going to do that, right?

With that said, create some type of customer retention campaign. Oftentimes it just means staying in contact with past customers, even if only once every few months, to let them know you are still thinking about them.

Social media and mobile campaigns are more great ways to spread the word on exclusive offers created especially for your best customers. It's time to get creative!

Below are some simple suggestions for making your customers feel appreciated (therefore increasing your customer satisfaction and retention levels):

- Offer a 'gift with purchase program' whether it is a small tangible item or a discount on a future purchase.

- Coupons are an affordable, effective, and an easy way to distribute your specials. (Note: If you choose coupons remember to code them in such a manner that you can track them upon their return to you. Gage your response rates and you will learn the best media avenues to use in the future).

- **"FREE"** is an attention-getting, powerful word. We love our freebies and samples! Who doesn't appreciate a small token of gratitude, even something insignificant and inexpensive. A free calendar or ink pen are still appreciated. People love promotional gifts plus they may have your business contact information printed on them.

- Consider offering free classes and events to your customers. This is a fantastic way to get them in the door especially if you provide a service or sell retail products.

  - ✓ TIP: Great businesses for this could include a craft or art supply shop, book store, floral shop, hardware store, pet care store, home improvement, cafe, hair salon, and so many more.

  - ✓ Highlight some type of do-it-yourself project using materials in your store (or charge a minimal fee for supplies). Offer light refreshments.

  - ✓ Bring in a guest speaker to educate them on a topic of interest. Think of the great topics that could be presented if you own an antique store. People love to hear about items from eras past.

✓ Special makeover events at a hair salon could be a hit. A pet groomer can offer tips on care of their pet's coat between grooming appointments.

✓ Once in your store, chances are they will purchase materials or products as well. Make a special deal for that day only.

In conclusion, know the *Big Three Mistakes*. They are crucial to the success of your business. To review:

1. **Solely marketing to gain new customers**

2. **Not effectively using cross-sells, up-sells or packaged-deal selling techniques**

3. **Underestimating the lifetime value of a loyal customer**

As an added bonus, you will find worksheet pages at the end of each chapter. They will help you collect and organize your thoughts and ideas for your own marketing strategies.

WORKBOOK – CHAPTER 1

List your five most popular selling items (product or service):

1.

2.

3.

4.

5.

What **Cross-Sell** could you create for each? (Remember the '*would you like fries with that*?' example). These may be the same for each item.

1.

2.

3.

4.

5.

List **Up-Sells** you could create for each. (An Up-Sell is a premium version of what they stand to already purchase). Again, these may be the same for each item, but list it anyway.

1.

2.

3.

4.

5.

List items, products or services that would make up a good **Packaged-Deal**. (Example: Items that can be grouped together such as shampoo and conditioner with a deep conditioning treatment added in as a package).

1.

2.

3.

4.

5.

Let's put a lifetime dollar value on your average customer:

First, determine how frequently they visit your store on average. Decide on the average frequency and multiply that component to determine how many times **per year** they visit your store. Use your best guess here. List another frequency amount if not listed here and total the annual visits. This isn't exact but it can give you an idea.

Weekly? _____ x 52 weeks in a year **- OR -**

Monthly? _____ x 12 months in a year **- OR –**

Customized: _____

A. **Total average visits per year**: _____

> The optimal average **age** of your ideal customer is _____.
> So, ideally, how many more years will this customer visit your store?

B. **How many more years?** _____

C. The **average dollar amount** spent per purchase per visit to your store? $_____

Multiply the number of annual visits **(A)** by the average dollar amount per visit **(C)**:

A _____ x **C** $_____ = **D** $_____ (Annual receipts)

Multiply the amount of annual receipts **(D)** by the number of years you anticipate this customer to visit your store **(B)**.

D $ _____ x **B** = _____ This is the lifetime value of your loyal customer.

The Lifetime Value of My Ideal Loyal Customer Is: $_____

Chapter Two

CENTER OF INFLUENCE MARKETING

I will go out on a limb and say that traditional methods of advertising can be a significant waste of money if you are not careful. Why? Because traditional advertising will land you traditional results, or none at all, if not carefully targeted. You do not become an industry leader or a dominant presence in your community by doing things the same way as everyone else.

To this I can only say: If you are not willing to be extraordinary, then you will have to settle for ordinary results.

Unbelievable to me, there are still small business owners choosing to advertise in the Yellow Pages. The only reason I can remotely conjure up for this is that the merchant simply doesn't know what else to do. It is becoming crystal clear that phone book advertising has become obsolete. The masses are now using the internet and smart phones for their information resources and that's where we must focus a sizable component of your marketing strategies. Today we can instantly look up any person or business in the world at the tap of a button. It is crucial that businesses find their footing in the mainstream of today's new mobile and social marketing technologies or, unfortunately, risk getting left behind by their competition. We the People "Google" everything, you know.

Almost all print ads look about the same these days. Take a look. Could it be because they are all designed by the same person or company? Of course, this means that each ad is (by definition) traditional, meaning nondescript. Blah. I want you to know that you do not have to simply get in line here and follow blindly.

Newspaper advertising, though better than some options, is also lagging behind. But again, almost all the ads oftentimes look the same. They are designed by the same person or groups of people. If everything looks the same, everyone gets the same type of results. Not to mention there are online options available now, too.

Finally, consider this: When advertising in traditional arenas, you are advertising in the *same places as your competitors*, so in essence you are competing with them again in that space. With no disrespect intended, because I highly respect and regard anyone who can successfully brave the business world, but that's kind of silly, isn't it? I would rather advertise in a vacuum where I know at least one person would see the ad—even if it's only me. At least there I would be the only choice.

My point is this: Locate your customers and stand out and away from your competition so *you* are the one they find.

Today's marketplace is extremely competitive. You have to break through barriers, fight your way out of the box, and start thinking while you are out there. Remember? Lose the box.

I fashion myself as a collector of good and creative ideas. I look for those unique ways of promoting and advertising that do not garner just ordinary results, but rather extraordinary results instead.

What I am about to show you is going to give you a far greater return than traditional advertising ever will. It will also dramatically enhance the relationship you have with your fellow business owners. It could make others think that you are some sort of genius because of your innovation in marketing and respected community relations.

I am talking about something called the *Center of Influence Marketing*, and how it can take on many faces.

Here's the premise: Instead of hunting down your ideal prospects, what would happen if you connected with noncompeting merchants (where your customers are known to frequent) and worked out a mutually beneficial relationship with them?

Physical Locations:

Go where your customers are already hanging out instead of randomly, hopefully, and painstakingly picking them up one by one in the newspaper, on the television or radio, or in the phone book.

Here is what you can do: Identify several different businesses where your ideal customers frequent. Then construct an offer that will allow you to siphon those ideal customers off into your own sales funnel.

Let's take a second to talk about *targeted marketing* strategies. Say you and I each owned a pizza parlor. You need only one competitive advantage and you could destroy me and win every single customer if you played your cards right. Targeted marketing isolates and focuses your efforts on singling out those who are hungriest for whatever it is that you offer.

Let me make it real for you. Let's return to the retail flooring business. Think of people who buy flooring—what else do they tend to need that complements that?

Many people who need flooring may also need paint. What would happen if you had a majority of the paint stores sending the customers who needed flooring your way?

If I wanted to approach a small business to offer my marketing consultation services, where could I go? One possibility would be to start with local accountants. They help business owners with their bookkeeping and taxes, and they know who the start-ups are, too.

I could also approach the heads of trade associations of which small business owners would be a member (like the Chamber of Commerce or networking groups, for example), and volunteer to give a free talk or lecture where I would share my expertise on my chosen craft.

I have seen many an eye glaze over when I suggested this Public speaking has consistently ranked number one in the list of what people fear most. I feel it is important to say this: Do not let the whole speech idea make your knees buckle and your mouth go dry.

You *know* your business; you *know* what you're talking about. Use your expertise to an advantage and take the opportunity to help your potential customers. You are the expert. Imagine everyone in the audience wearing lipstick and a diaper. (TIP: Do not imagine them naked. You may not be able to look them in the eye again). You've got this. I will say it again: You are the expert here.

Remind yourself why you are there and speaking to begin with. If feeling 'salesy' is uncomfortable to you, remember that you are not selling them anything; you are there to deliver information they find beneficial. You are there to serve your community and to be of service as well.

I highly recommend getting involved with local networking groups and other professional or trade groups of peers where individuals offer training and information sessions. Not only is the education worth every penny, the reach of networking opportunities can surprise you. You meet like-minded people and get new customers, too.

I would also go to attorneys that help people form corporations and who specialize in helping small businesses. Volunteer to speak at seminars. Host a roundtable discussion or an open house for getting folks together. These are proven strategies that work well for gaining respect, visibility and establishing expertise.

Do you see what I'm doing here? I am finding a complementary, non-competitive business entity that already attracts the 'hungry' customers. Instead of having to find those customers myself, I am leveraging on the efforts of others.

It needs to make sense for them to refer customers to you before they will actually do so. What is an easy way to do this? Why not say, "Hey, I know from time to time you have customers that also need my services. Let's partner up…combine our resources."

In other words, send customers to *them* in return. It could be as simple as creating a promotional flyer to put in their business, and they do likewise to distribute at your business. Now it's a referral revolving door and more importantly, it is a win-win situation. You are going to find it surprisingly easy to do this. Your colleagues in other businesses are looking for options, just as you are, and they welcome any creative ideas they can get. And to partner with someone they trust? Priceless.

Begin by thinking of five complementary types of industries. Pick the top three businesses in each of them. Now you could have a list of fifteen businesses to approach.

Secondly, create your irresistible offer for these businesses. You could come up with something quite enticing that answers their number one question: *What's in it for me?*

Consider creating a unique offer just for *their* customers exclusively. It could be a discount, or something extra they get for free for which would normally be charged. This way, the *what's in it for me?* question is answered by the fact that their customers receive special treatment and will appreciate them even more. It looks like the owner went to bat and negotiated a special deal with you, just for them.

How many businesses could you do this with? As many as you like! This can help you acquire new customers, especially when you combine this with referral marketing. You could easily get ten businesses that were complementary to yours to promote for you for some sort of incentive and be respected in the business community for reciprocating.

For some, it might just be that you place some flyers at the counter that includes a special freebie coupon just for their customers, and that's okay. For other businesses it might be a customer exchange. You send customers their way if they send customers to you.

In any case, realize the importance behind this—most of the cost for customer acquisition will only be paid after the customer is acquired. You get referrals because you refer. You can't beat that.

This truly takes the risk out of advertising, because you will only pay for it when it works. Not a bad deal!

Virtual Locations:

Welcome to the future. The dawn of the social and mobile marketing era has arrived, and it is here to stay.

Within this realm of express communication, social media, mass text, email messaging, and optimized mobile websites have become the hottest and most significant of marketing opportunities simply because of the little trend called the cellular telephone and, to a larger and more significant degree, the smart phone and tablets.

According to the Pew Research Center, about ninety percent of the adult American population now own a cell phone and the vast majority of those are smart phones. Americans love our cell phones. Most of us keep our phones within personal reach at all times—day and night. Many of us have done away with our traditional landlines and rely solely on our cell phones and mobile devices.

Let's talk about the virtual world of mobile marketing. Your customers' time spent on mobile devices is rising faster than time spent on any other form of multimedia, and that includes the desktop internet. The statistics are overwhelming, and to *not* take full advantage of these vast and amazing opportunities...? I can't comprehend.

The use of cell phones and instant access to the internet has certainly created a landmark shift in business marketing today. Mobile application (app) usage has increased over six percent year over year, whether for reading email, shopping, obtaining information such as the news, downloading music and videos, accessing business and finance opportunities and productivity. The lion's share of time is now spent on social media engagement such as Facebook, Twitter, Instagram, Pinterest, and LinkedIn to name a few. Music, media and entertainment share a significant portion of how time is spent online via mobile devices. Is your presence there?

Today there are even more devices emerging onto center stage. Smart TV, smart watches, smart wristbands. There is payday associated with riding this wave of advertising opportunities. It is here that your customers have taken up residence in their virtual locations. It only makes sense to meet them here. Go where they are, remember?

Mobile marketing is a hot ticket in the technology buzz that helps attract more customers—customers that spend more money and do it more frequently. Consumers using a mobile browser are further down the purchasing funnel than website browsers and almost seventy percent of them proceed to make the call or go visit a store.

How does it work? By various means, such as by connecting with your customers through SMS (text) message marketing, optimized mobile websites, use of pertinent and targeted keywords for online searching purposes and via mobile advertising.

Consider a text messaging (SMS) campaign for your best clients. It has been proven that text messaging gets almost twenty times more response rate than that of opening an email. Many of us do not read every email message we receive on a daily basis, and there is no guarantee that we will read any specific email initially when there are literally dozens or more waiting in our cluttered in-boxes. Studies revealed that text messages have an astounding ninety-seven percent open rate. It is a no-brainer to be *virtually* everywhere your customers are by using mass text messaging or social media engagement.

Using Social Media for Local Advertising

The key to a successful text advertising strategy is to capture local customers (whom have opted in as your loyal customer) in a focused, timely and consistent manner. There are applications that have been designed specifically for this and they are user friendly.

Is your restaurant slow on Monday nights? Send out a virtual coupon via a text blast at 4:30p.m. and enjoy a larger crowd for dinner that evening. Did your retail store recently receive a new shipment of a wildly popular item? Send your preferred customers a special discount if they come in to purchase today. With a text advertising VIP Club or Preferred Customer Program, you don't have to *hope* that your customers will come in today...you can *entice* them to!

Here is where it gets good. The days of mobile marketing are just beginning. We are merely cave people at this point—and we have just discovered fire! Less than ten percent of businesses have tapped into this next big trend but make no mistake, more of them are becoming hip to these methods every day. They must in order to remain competitive. Now is the perfect time for you to get the jump on your competition.

Text messaging has become the number one use for mobile phones—more than phone calls, more than emails, web-surfing, and even social media combined (though social media such as Facebook and Twitter certainly claim great advertising stakes for your business, too). Today's savvy business owner has social media on their radar screen.

Most text messages are read within an hour. Think about it this way: Do you text? How many text messages do you receive—and ignore? If you are like most people, probably none.

Text messages are almost impossible to ignore because when they arrive on your cell phone, they are the ONLY thing visible on the screen. A text message claims its unique space—exclusively and alone. They see the text and nothing but the text. To boot, the text notification envelope stays on the screen until the recipient accesses the text (this also acts as a nice reminder).

A text message marketing campaign might work like this: Your customers opt-in to your text message campaigns by texting a predetermined 'short code' or 'long code' to a specified number arranged by your marketing professional. For instance, if you run a pizza parlor you could post signs or table tents in your establishment that say, "Text PIZZA to 42474 to join our club and receive coupons and special offers from us!" It is important to note that in order to comply with federal law we must also let the customer know that standard text rates may apply and opt-out instructions are offered should they wish to do so.

Staying with the food service industry example, you could blast out this bulk text campaign:

> *Show this text to your server & receive a Free Appetizer on Tuesday between 4p.m. and 6p.m. Forward this to friends and they can enjoy it, too!*

Be aware that about one in five business-texted offers get forwarded to the recipients' friends and colleagues thus increasing your response rate. If you make the offer special enough or enticing enough, trust me, they will come (and oftentimes they bring friends).

Contrary to past beliefs, it's not just those crazy teenagers and twenty-somethings driving this trend any more. It's *all* active people. Business people, parents, students, the butcher, the baker and the… well, you get the picture. It is all of us. It's probably you, and for sure heck-fire, it's me, too.

In a tough economy, your customers appreciate a good deal at their favorite establishments and your bottom line will appreciate the added business. It is widely known that American families enjoy eating out several times a week, meaning they are going to eat *somewhere*…so why not meet up at *your* place?

Send out that text blast and jog your loyal customer's memory. Remind them that you are there—ready and waiting to serve them well.

Make Sure Your Website is Mobile Optimized

In addition to text message marketing there is the ability for websites to become optimized especially for mobile phones that are specifically targeted toward local businesses. Available applications, known as apps, abound by the thousands. There are companies that specialize in customized app creation for your business. It is very effective and more advanced that text message marketing with more advantages, but apps are not for everyone.

Uninformed small business owners may hesitate when it comes to securing a mobile website for their business. Missing the unlimited opportunities afforded you by implementing mobile optimized sites could be perceived as dismissing the needs and convenience of your customers. It is very important to offer a user friendly mobile site that is fast and inexpensive for the customer to load. We are a mobile society and to be clear, local customers are doing very specific mobile searches looking to fill their wants and needs. Trust me, if the customer can't find you, they *will* find your competition. Rest easy knowing that many websites now come with a mobile optimized plugin automatically. Test your site frequently by visiting it on your phone. This way you see what your customers see and can tweak it as needed.

Appreciate the fact that the mobile surfer is seldom just browsing with no particular place to go. He usually has a specific goal when searching on his mobile device—to find what he is looking for whether it be price comparisons, directions on how to get to your store, or how to purchase your product or service. The most important aspects, however, are the ability to be found in the first place, the site's content and how it is presented.

The needs and behaviors of a mobile internet surfer differ from an desktop surfer. Statistics show that mobile surfers are further down the purchase funnel and stand poised and ready to take specific buying action such as calling you or visiting your store after viewing your information on their mobile browser.

When making the decision on whether to invest in making your business visible in the vast mobile world, consider these four fierce facts:

1. **Customers are looking for your services** (or those of your competitor if they can't find *you*!) on their mobile devices, whether you have a mobile site or not.

2. **Customers will find your competitors' sites** if your website is difficult to find or difficult to navigate. Guaranteed. Remember my KISS Marketing System? Yes, simplicity wins.

3. **Your business could be perceived as being behind the times** if lacking the latest mobile technology.

4. **A misinformed customer is an unhappy one.** By choosing no mobile optimization for your website, understand what you are losing. When the customer attempts to open your website in their mobile browser he may be greeted with a slow download with a wacky layout making it impossible to find the information he seeks. In frustration, he clicks away and on to see what your competitor's mobile site can do for him. I have personally done this many, many times.

Mobile Advertising

When you have a mobile website, you can utilize Search Engine Optimization (SEO) to broaden your brand's exposure. This means using specific and targeted keywords in all of your written content to specifically describe your business making it easier for your customers and potential customers to locate you online. Identify and use these keywords liberally throughout your websites, social media, and blogs. Everywhere!

One way to delve into keywords is to go to the Google Keyword Planner and type in specific keywords to describe your business, product or service. Review the words and phrases that come up and target your keywords accordingly. Use these keywords on your media properties. This means your website and on all social media sites. These are what we call searchable terms, meaning what one would type in to a browser to find you.

Something else to consider are display banners and inserts within text messaging, your own app, and internet searches. Any combination of these forms of mobile advertising will invite a consumer to engage in various forms of mobile media: SMS text, mobile web, apps and click to call. Best of all, the price for mobile advertising is a fraction of the cost of desktop paid advertising campaigns. I caution you to seek the assistance of a marketing professional unless you are very well versed in these types of marketing measures.

Savvy business owners today now realize that they need to have an online presence. They know that their online presence needs to be found. And they know that their online presence must be trusted.

Let's apply what we know so far:

In general, targeted phone book advertising is obsolete; newspapers are choking for readers; billboards get ignored; television and radio ads cost a small fortune (with zero guarantee that your targeted audience is even paying attention). With advanced capabilities that come with your satellite television options, many of us are simply skipping over the commercials. I do. So, what is a small business owner to do? How do you get to top of mind for your customers and potential customers?

Most local business owners are unsure of how to fill the advertising gap that leaves them digging deeper for innovative ideas every day. If you feel like you have already dug your way to China and don't know where to turn, read on. By adding mobile and social marketing in cooperation with optimized mobile websites to your marketing and advertising repertoire, you have found your unique ticket to exclusivity!

The KiSS System
Keep. It. Simple. Stupid.

WORKBOOK – CHAPTER 2

What **types** of **physical locations** might your ideal client frequent?

List several businesses where your ideal customer may frequent:

Examples: A carwash client may frequent an auto parts store

A restaurant customer may frequent a grocery store

A customer getting new flooring may also need paint

If one buys a new mattress, they may need new bedding

List local groups that you can join to network and market your services and may have the opportunity to speak.

Get involved yourself or send a representative!

Example: Chamber of Commerce, networking groups, other local businesses, community and charity organizations.

This exercise will help you identify some potential businesses that you could consider partnering with and with whom you could exchange customers. Refer to page 32 if you need to review.

List 5 complementary *types* of *industries* that your customers may frequent. For example: Everyone goes to a grocery or a hair salon regardless of your particular industry type.

1.

2.

3.

4.

5.

Now pick the top three **local businesses** in each industry type

Industry #1

1.

2.

3.

Industry #2

1.

2.

3.

Industry #3

1.

2.

3.

Industry #4

1.

2.

3.

Industry #5

1.

2.

3.

You now have at least fifteen businesses with whom you could potentially partner. These are easy calls to make. Business owners love to connect with others to help market their business.

Are you ready to add some spark to a slow day? List a few sample ideas for text or social media blast announcing a customer appreciation special. Remember, be creative!

Chapter Three

HOW TO FIND CUSTOMERS FOR LIFE

Imagine that there was a huge gold mine out in your backyard, right under your nose. We're talking millions of dollars' worth of gold. Would that make you rich? Nope. Not if you didn't know about it. You could live your entire life sitting on a massive fortune and be none the wiser.

However, if I told you about it and showed you beyond a shadow of doubt that there was indeed gold located there you could mine it to find it. You could be abundantly wealthy.

In most businesses there exists a situation like the gold mine example above. Small business owners are sometimes sitting on a potential fortune, but they don't realize it. The tricks of the trade involve getting the customers to mentally think of your business first when it's your special services they seek. We need you to be the situation of Top of Mind Awareness for your customers. This means it is *your* business that comes to mind when they desire or need the type of product or service your business provides.

In this chapter I am going to share with you perhaps the single most effective strategy for mining the hidden gold that is likely to exist in your business.

- ✓ **First, know your market inside and out**. Know it better than your competition. Learn who your customers are before you spend a dime on directing any advertising to them. Talk to the movers and shakers in your local community; read your trade journals as they are filled with useful information; watch the news for consumer buying trends.

- ✓ **A second proven marketing strategy is to study your competition**. Once you have a good picture of who they are and what their business is about (their store layout, pricing structure, advertising strategies, return policies, product services—or lack thereof), you can determine their vulnerabilities and cash in on them for your own business. Don't be shy on this one.

- ✓ **Third, socially network within local business and community groups as well as with your competitors**. You might be surprised how loose-lipped they can become by saying too much about their upcoming products, specials or services.

In the past, I have suggested to some of my clients that it could be wise to construct a focus group consisting of a few of their best customers. The group is asked to discuss what they like or don't like about their products or services. Ask targeted questions and you will receive targeted information in return. The group could tell you quite a bit about your company, and even more about your competition in the process.

This method is great for local market research. I have personally used this method in creating marketing strategies in my own businesses and I find it to be invaluable. It makes the chosen few feel much more important and maintains their loyalty to your brand because they have established a sense of ownership at that point. This may not be the scientific approach, but it works.

Take advantage of the competitive edge your customers can offer, simply by seeking out their insight. Having this type of information in your hip pocket can be powerfully effective!

The "Forgotten Rule" of an Obscure Italian Economist

In 1906 a man by the name of Vilfredo Pareto discovered something unusual about the Italian economy. He found that eighty percent of the wealth was controlled by twenty percent of the population. We know it today as the 80/20 Rule.

Was this just an anomaly? Turns out it was not. In Britain he found the same thing to be true and went on to have the same findings in most all economies he examined. But what is interesting is that this unequal distribution exists outside of economies as well. For instance, studies have shown in general that:

- 80% of traffic accidents are committed by 20% of drivers

- 80% of crimes are committed by 20% of the population

- 80% of a company's output comes from 20% of its employees, and most importantly of all...

- 80% of your profits come from only 20% of your customers!

This rule almost always rings true. So, what does this mean for you—and for your business? Simply put: If you can isolate who your "twenty percenters" are, and come up with a marketing plan that will attract more customers like them, then create additional products, services and offers for them, then you should be able to easily add twenty percent to your bottom line profits in very short order.

Where to Start

Depending upon your type of business, in an ideal situation, you have probably kept track of your past customers' purchases. You at least know what your top selling products are. What you want to do now is go through and isolate those customers who have spent the *most* money with you. These are the ones that know, like, and trust your business.

Obviously, that does not necessarily mean that they are your most profitable customers. They are just your highest grossing customers. Unfortunately, gross does not always mean more profits. However, it is a good place to start.

After you find your highest grossing customers, analyze your profit margin on those customers, to narrow it down even more. To make it easy for you, come up with your twenty *highest grossing* customers, and out of those twenty, arrange them in order of most profitable.

Now take your twenty *most profitable* customers and analyze them. What we are looking for are trends of demographics and psychographics. In other words, you are trying to isolate their buying "culture," if you will. Many times, you can glean this information simply by having brief conversations with them. I have also used survey cards in which I ask for their email address and communicate that way as well.

Demographics are things such as:

- size of household
- annual income earned
- age
- gender
- geographical location

Psychographics are:

- clubs they belong to
- hobbies and interests
- values and opinions
- shopping habits
- lifestyle & other behavior attributes

Another activity is to create a customer avatar. An avatar is a fictional character that represents your ideal customer and helps you understand their buying habits. How can this be helpful to you? Let's say you analyze your results and find out that your most profitable customers are typically:

- aged 25-45
- have two to three children
- are married
- live on the northeast side of town
- make somewhere between $75,000 to $100,000 a year
- are active in the community; especially involved with charitable events
- typically play a lot of golf and/or tennis
- take two to three vacations a year

Note: There is a client avatar exercise in the workbook at the back of this chapter, but if you would like to further explore how to create your ideal customer's avatar, I have included a free downloadable worksheet on website. Visit www.thekissmarketingsystem.com.

That is some valuable information! For starters, did you know you can rent a list in your area with those specifications? Yes, for a fee you could get a list of all the people in your city that are between twenty-five and fifty, living in a certain zip code, making an annual income of $75,000 to $100,000 a year. And that's just a few of the "selects" you can specify. You can even go deeper if you wish.

These are the type of prospects you want to concentrate on with your marketing dollars. While past results do not necessarily guarantee future behavior, they are about as good an indicator to go by as any. The point is, if that type of customer was profitable to you in the past, It stands to reason similar people who fit that description will also be extremely profitable for you now as well.

The best thing to do next is to create a direct mail campaign and send a letter to each name on your list making them an exclusive offer (unless you opted to utilize text, app or social media advertising whereas saving paper and postage budgets).

You want to write an advertisement that is personable, explains the benefits of your services, and makes a special introductory offer to get them back into your place of business. You can also add beneficial advertising information in your newsletter.

In your advertisements address things like golf and tennis, taking vacations, saying things that your identified demographics are known to associate with, and talk about charitable events. This helps build rapport with the prospect. You just have to tie those things to your sales message and special offer in some creative way.

That's just one simple example of how to make the 80/20 Rule work in your favor.

Here's an even better example: Look into your customer records of your most profitable customers and ask yourself, "What services and goods can I offer them that they don't currently have, but would be complementary to purchases they've made in the past?"

If someone is a very profitable customer to you, it usually means that they like doing business with you, need a lot of what you have to offer, trust you, and often think of you as the "go-to" solution (top of mind awareness) for problems related to your area of service and expertise.

If you have a good recommendation that could help bring them value to their life and fits perfectly for something you have offered them in the past, you're likely to be met with success.

There are several methods that will assist you in maximizing your efforts. Start with your top twenty customers. Write them each a personal letter. Start with letting them know that you were analyzing your past records and noticed that they have been a very good and valued customer. Then say you also noticed something that may be a benefit to them based on their past purchases. Add that since they have been such good customers, you are going to give them a special deal next time they come into the store and purchase something. Give them specific examples, such as:

"Thank you for purchasing (fill in the blank) from us in the past. We wanted to let you know that we have a new product that complements it perfectly. If you come in within the next two weeks I can give you a special deal of 30% off the regular price. This is just our way of saying Thank You for being such a valuable customer."

Another strategy to consider is the referral strategy. People typically hang around others who share their same values and beliefs. This is a perfect way to attract new customers who are likely to be just as profitable as those identified as your past most profitable customers.

In this case, send your best customers a letter and let them know that you're making them an "exclusive offer." Add that if they were to recommend someone to your business you will give their referrals a "preferred VIP discount" or "preferred VIP treatment" since they came from a highly valued source.

People love to refer when this is the case. It makes them look good in front of their friends. A lot of people find value in that. It is also great for you, because word of mouth advertising is some of the *best advertising* there is. And if you can just get these referrals into the door and have them start a buying relationship with you, chances are they will continue to buy from you in the future. Thus, you will get more than just a one-time purchase; you may get another customer for life with a high lifetime value. Then they tell their friends and you organically grow new loyal customers.

As a case in point on a personal level: After injuring my lower back while blow-drying my hair, (yeah, don't ask…) one of my employees referred me to a local business which happened to be owned by her cousin. This facility specialized in massage therapy and various spa services. Being in agony with any attempted movement, I made an appointment and hobbled in. After only two therapy sessions I was amazed at how much better my back felt—I could actually move without squeaking. (My husband said I made "squeaking noises" when I made any attempt at painful movement. Sexy, huh?)

After that I became a loyal customer, keeping a regular monthly appointment for a therapeutic and relaxing massage because I loved the benefits of massage. The price was right, the services were wonderful and I appreciated being treated like a valued customer. I started referring anyone that would listen to me to this business so that friends and acquaintances could enjoy the same satisfaction in which I reveled—not to mention that I received fifteen minutes *free* on my next massage as a 'thank you for the referral.'

That Christmas, to my surprise, I walked in for my regular appointment, and sitting on the counter was a beautifully presented gift basket filled with spa products—for *me!* The attached card spoke of the owner's appreciation for the referrals I had sent their way over the course of the year.

Needless to say, I know the value of customer loyalty. That was about ten years ago and I still feel special when I walk in. The owner of the shop was very approachable and open to suggestions and listened intently when we asked for a monthly "girlfriend special" which she soon initiated. To this day, my friend and I go every month (at *least* once) for a spa day. These are life's little necessities, you know. It's a rule. We can't break it.

My husband also tells me he thinks I make up the rules as I go along. Maybe. But I no longer squeak.

Make your customers feel special, my friend.

That's the bottom line.

WORKBOOK – CHAPTER 3

In this brief exercise, create your ideal customer avatar. An avatar is a fictional character that resembles your ideal customer. Feel free to create multiple avatars to help you better understand your customer's wants, needs, and pain points. This is a great way to explore your average client demographic. There is most likely no way you are privy to all of this information, but you can calculate generalities to identify your best client type.

Give your ideal customer a name:

How old is your ideal customer?

Marital status:

How many children / ages?

Where do they live?

About how much money do they make?

What are their hobbies?

Type of occupation?

What are their challenges?

What do they typically purchase when they come into your place of business?

What other product or service do you offer that would benefit them or complement their previous purchases?

What are their objections to making purchases at your place of business?

Address their issues: How can your product or service make their day better?

What are their hopes and dreams or goals?

List any other identifiers here:

Now write a paragraph summarizing your avatar(s):

Chapter Four

THE POWER OF WORD-OF-MOUTH MARKETING

The Referral Marketing Goldmine

Referrals are the least expensive, yet among the most effective, marketing tactics in the world. We are best advised to respect word of mouth advertising because that door can swing two ways—and one of those ways can hurt a business' reputation in the local community considerably. By delivering the services you promise, you keep your customers happy and they are delighted to share their good experiences with their extended family, friends and colleagues.

The idea is that you should be generating a substantial portion of your new customers by marketing to existing customers. You simply cannot put a price on the value of your existing loyal customer base.

Read that again. I'll wait.

There are several reasons why nurturing a referral program is the smart thing to do. First, quality attracts quality. Psychologists say that you are basically a combination of your five closest friends. In other words, people will refer people who are similar to them.

So, if you have a big spender, then guess what? They will most likely refer other big spenders. Every good customer should be actively pursued for a referral because they will usually generate other customers of equal quality and value.

Also, marketing is usually met with skepticism. That is mainly because you are often tooting your own horn in order to get the business. But what if someone else was tooting your horn for you?

Know this—people are more likely to believe in you if someone else endorses your qualities than if you brag about them yourself (as splendid as your qualities may be).

What you are really doing is leveraging off someone else's credibility. People who take the recommendations of their friends are now coming to you with a preconceived notion that you are already quality—before you even have to open your mouth.

Finally, word of mouth marketing is a laser target marketing strategy. Basically, you are only going to be getting people who are already in the market for the type of services you are offering. Mass marketing does not have this effect. If you run an ad on television, you are targeting every single person who watches TV. Period.

Adversely, with referral marketing, you are getting only people who are already a great match to your products or services. This means your closing rate will go up without much effort on your part. You are just getting people who are already more likely to say "yes" before they even enter into the store.

Note an important rule of thumb when it comes to referral marketing. Every good customer should get at least three direct chances to refer someone else to you. If you are providing excellent services, this won't be difficult to achieve. I have found to get the best results you have to ask someone three times to make a referral on your behalf. If you do nothing else, you should do this.

To make it more effective, there are two crucial tasks at hand: Make it (a) *easy* for them to refer and (b) make it *worthwhile* for them to refer. This is a double-edged sword designed to leverage your efforts much more in-depth than you could believe possible. I am going to show you how to do all of this and more as you create your stress-free marketing strategies with your own referral systems.

The Referral System: Step By Step

First, get your metrics in order. How much money can you afford to spend on marketing for the next month? Whatever it is, devote the largest portion of it to your referral marketing.

Step one, identify your budget. Of course, much of this depends upon your type of business services and categories.

The specific plan I am going to lay out to you is going to cost around $8 per person to perform. If you have a budget of $800 for targeted marketing, then you can reach 100 people.

Start small and scale up. Do not spend too much money upfront until you get back some reliable figures, and you can do some testing. Since this is a system, every dollar you spend will be tracked and traced back to determine the return on your investment.

Here's how it works. Remember, we are mostly addressing small and local businesses in this book, so there is a chance you would have access to customer address. If not, there are other ways. There are direct mailing lists you can rent or purchase. Direct mail is pretty effective as it can get past your customer's front door. It may be very much worth your while to enlist such a service. Consider having your clients sign up for your newsletter. You can require an email and physical address on the subscription form.

Say someone comes in and purchases an item or service from you and appears pretty satisfied with their gains. This is the perfect time to ask for a referral. If you do not have access to their address, have an attractive card with a special offer ready to go and add it to their shopping bag. You thank them and make it easy for them to refer a friend while making it worth their while, too.

The most important part is that you have enabled it to be in their best interest to refer others to you. For that to happen, first and foremost you must have provided quality and value. I am going to assume you are performing good service and living up to your end of the deal—this time and every time.

Second, consider that small gifts work wonders (remember the gift basket from my favorite spa?). The best kind of gifts are those that either cost me nothing or very little but have a huge perception of value. Without a doubt, there is one gift I can consistently create for basically nothing, and it always does the trick.

Coupon Books

This is the Center of Influence Marketing theory at its finest. It works like this: Approach various business owners and colleagues and tell them that you want to help make sure your mutual customers continue to shop locally. (You could even engage a college student to help make the initials calls for you). Go back to the list you created in the workbook at the end of Chapter Two.

As a thank-you token for your customers, you would like to gift them with coupons or special offers from other local merchants. This equates to providing your customers with added value while keeping their patronage local in cooperation with your fellow business managers.

At that point, simply ask your colleagues if they have any coupons or any exclusive offers that they would like to contribute to your "customer gift book." Cross-marketing with other businesses complementary to yours usually works quite well.

Almost every business owner you talk to will want to take you up on this joint venture. Why? Simple! Because most businesses are not good at doing their own marketing, and to make up for it they always have a special offer or are willing to do anything if it means getting a few more customers in the store.

You can obtain as few as ten unique coupon offers to make a great gift book. This could be accomplished within a few hours. There are easy design templates available to download on the internet or you can visit www.thekissmarketingsystem.com for this and other resources.

Now you have a nice gift that you can give to anybody who sends a referral your way. How much did this cost you? Merely the cost to print the coupons and mail them or hand deliver them. You just made a gift of high perceived value (everybody loves discounts) that costs you about a dollar to create and a few hours of creative glisten equity. It is worth the while.

Let's consider what the first referral letter could look like. Of course, feel free to customize this with your own business brand. It might look something like this:

Dear Carol Customer,

We want to say thank you for doing business with us. If there is anything you need from (our services – fill in the blank) in the future, please do not hesitate to call.

You may not realize this, but the lifeline of our business comes from referrals. If you happen to know anyone who would benefit from our services, I would be extremely honored to help them in any way.

If the person you refer becomes our customer, I will send both of you my special VIP customer gift book, which has discounts totaling over $250 (or other amount) from various local businesses!

It's easy to refer someone to us. I've enclosed two of my business cards with your name written on the back. Please give them to anyone you think could use our services. Just have them present the business card when they come in, so we know it was you that referred them!

Anyway, I just wanted to say thanks again for doing business with us!

With Sincere Appreciation,
Shana McQueen
Business Owner

There is a lot of psychology that is going on in this first letter that I don't want you to miss. First, it is personal and it is sincere. How many businesses have you bought something from in the last sixty days from which you received a personal thank you letter in the mail? One or two, you say? None? Amazing.

Imagine the kind of impact that your letter has when it lands in your customer's mailbox. Significant impact. It says you care. It says you remember them. Do you remember why most people leave a service provider?

Sadly, some pass away. Some may have to relocate. Others leave because of an unresolved complaint or situation. A handful will be stolen away by a competitor. Add all those up, and guess what?

It usually only comes to thirty-two percent of all total customers who leave you. So, what about the other sixty-eight percent?

They leave simply because you have never taken the time or initiative to recognize them as something more than a customer.

Pop quiz: It is a busy day in your store or office, but as usual, issues abound. Choosing to deal with only one of the following, which would it be?

    a.   An unresolved complaint

    b.   A direct competitor in your store trying to steal your customer

    c.   The opportunity to let a recent customer know you care about them

Which would you address? You are best served to choose the third option because remember, roughly only nine percent leave because of competition, and only fourteen percent leave because of unresolved complaints.

If you do nothing else but keep in contact with your past customers and treat them as your friends and acknowledge them occasionally, you will be putting the golden lasso on the remaining sixty-eight percent of your customers. This will allow you to keep selling to them again and again. That builds your brand and customer loyalty. So, please—if they give you their loyalty, treat them like royalty.

First, if you get nothing else out of the referral letter, you will get personal communication that will separate you from ninety percent of all businesses and almost every single one of your competitors.

The second thing the referral letter does is conveys your expectations. You *expect* all your customers to refer. Most people don't refer simply because they don't know you want them to refer. In fact, I have had customers come up and tell my clients, "Heck, I thought you already had enough customers...I didn't know you could take on more."

You should have seen the business owner slap his forehead on that one. It left a mark.

Once people know that you *want* them to refer their friends, you automatically increase the chances they *will* refer—even if it isn't immediate. Again, I have had people hold on to business cards for two or three years before they gave one to someone else.

Notice the casual tone of our referral letter. People prefer doing business with friends, and not faceless corporations.

Finally, it shows you care. The above letter basically says, "I know you're busy and I know you have to look out for your self-interests. That's why I have gone the extra mile to make it in your own self-interest to refer to me."

Ideally, you don't want to take the above letter word for word. You want to fill in "our services" with your actual services and so forth. But you have complete permission to take most of the above verbatim and use it.

But don't stop there. After the first letter has been sent, wait a couple of weeks or so. If you haven't gotten a referral from them go for contact number two.

Dear Carol Customer,

We have delivered several of our VIP gift books in the last few weeks to valued customers who referred their friends to us. To make sure you don't miss out on your own special gift book, I have enclosed two more business cards with your name on the back, just in case you need them.

Give these to a friend in need, and we will mail your customer gift book right away!

Once again, thank you for being our valued customer, and I hope that we can continue to provide you with more great service in the years to come.

Thanks again,
Shana M.
Business Owner

Here is what I know about marketing: One-shot (single contact) advertising is not very effective. It's not that people don't want to act on your offers. A lot of them do. What happens is that the details of hectic day-to-day living get in the way, and what they intend on doing ends up getting pushed to the back of their mind. We all know how that goes, only too well. Am I right?

What this letter does is thank them again, puts you in front of them again, and basically lets them off the hook. It wasn't their fault. You know and respect the fact that they are busy, too!

It gives you another excuse to send them two more business cards. It also offers some social proof that "everybody else is referring" and makes it more the thing to do.

Each time we track these campaigns, we usually find these types of responses:

- 3% to refer off the first letter

- 4% to refer off the second letter

- 2% to refer off the third, if you choose to follow up again.

In any case, all mailings are profitable. If we had stopped after the first letter, we would have gotten a mere 3% response rate. But instead we got 9% total! In most scenarios, it almost always plays out that the second letter will work the best. Who knows why; it just does.

I don't want you to confuse the technique with the strategy. This truly works because:

- It puts you in front of them two or three times

- It conveys the expectation that they will refer a friend

- It is personal, relaxed and friendly

- It is very easy to do

- It is in their best interest to put it to use; who doesn't appreciate a good deal?

You don't even have to do the coupon or gift book. Sometimes I'll just purchase tickets for a special upcoming local event, golf, movie, or event complimentary dinners at a good restaurant—anything your demographic may enjoy. You will need to decide on your method of obtaining each entrant's information. This could be a jar for them to insert their business card or an opt in form to subscribe to your newsletter. Use any way that is appropriate for your business type.

Lastly, a few pointers:

Make your letters look like personal letters. This means when you design the layout, don't put a fancy "brochure" feel into it. Just picture how you would design the letter if you were going to sit down and write someone a personal note.

When you get this system in place, you'll get some numbers. You might find for every five customers you do this for, you get one referral in the next thirty days. Okay, do that math—let's say your average sale netted you $100 in profit for each of the five customers. And let's say when you deduct all marketing expenses for creating and mailing the letters, it cost you $100. That's a 5 to 1 return on investment! Try getting that with other types of advertising.

This type of marketing also allows you to perform what is referred to as split-tests. What would happen if you altered the gift? You can literally test every element you want to learn what is working and what is not working. This means you can figure out the exact combination of steps for getting the greatest return on your advertising investment.

The KiSS System

Keep. It. Simple. Stupid.

WORKBOOK – CHAPTER 4

Describe three techniques you will use to get referrals in your particular business scenario. Train your staff as well.

1.

2.

3.

Craft your *Thank You* letter. If you don't have access to their mailing address, consider having them ready to slip into the customer's shopping bag or invest in direct mailing lists. You could also create brief survey cards and ask for the client's physical address and/or email address. Ask for their cell phone number and get permission to text them your specials. They have to approve or opt in.

Organize and create your special VIP Coupon Books. Revisit your list of potential business partners and invite them to contribute. It's a win-win! Below you will find dedicated journal space provided to collect your notes and information:

Jot Your Business Contact Numbers and Notes Here:

Chapter Five

OVERCOMING CUSTOMER RESISTANCE

How many of the people who walk into your business, or who take an interest in your products and services, end up making a purchase as opposed to those to who leave without making a purchase? As you know, in sales this is called a closing rate.

To manage any activity, you must first measure it. That way you know where you stand in terms of productivity, so you know what you need to do make improvements.

Here is an important question you need to answer: If ten prospects are interested in doing business with you, on average how many out of them end up doing business with you?

The percentage itself is not important. In stores with a lot of traffic, you can convert one out of ten and be fine. I had a client with a website where they converted one out of every one-hundred and it was enough for them to make a good return on their investment. It takes hardly any time or effort. In some businesses, you need five of the ten to purchase just to have a chance at making a profit.

While the actual percentage may not be that important, it is important is to know how to improve your percentages to a more acceptable or desirable range. If you get five out of ten people to make a purchase, do the math and see how much more you would make if you got six out of ten. Since they are already coming through your door, most of the work is done. You are just looking for those "little things" to get more people converted into customers.

There are a variety of ways to improve your closing rate and some are more complicated than others. I always look for the 80/20 factor in any given task. In other words, I am looking for that one or two key things that will make most of the difference between someone purchasing and not. Here is some insight to help you discover one vital fact that gives you most of your results.

Do you know what three criteria are required before a prospect becomes a customer? Knowing this will give you the answer you need. Here are the three all important components:

Criteria #1: They have to want what you offer.

Criteria #2: They must have money to purchase it.

Criteria #3: They need to believe that you will come through on your end of the deal.

The more inclined they are to already want what you have the easier it is to sell to them. The more money they have set aside for making consumer purchases, the easier it is to the sell to them. The more they believe that you will deliver on your offer, the easier it is to sell to them.

I have before me a phone book with Yellow Page ads. I'm going to flip through it and quote some phrases. Here are just a few (and a sample of skeptical consumer thoughts that may accompany the ads):

- **Dependable & Quality Service:** A typical savvy potential customer is thinking: *"Prove it, pal."*

- **Value, Service & Convenience:** This is meaningless, and everybody knows it. We may think: *"Convenience for whom—you or me?"*

- **Friendly Service:** Once again, consumers have heard this ad nauseum, and think: *"Yeah, right! I've heard that song before."*

- **In Business Over 100 Years:** *Longevity is great, but doesn't guarantee current technology, right?"*

In other words, these are hollow phrases of puffery that everybody uses. It is so easy to make these claims, and blindly saying them has come to mean so very little. In my own experience, I have called a business whose Yellow Page ad touted "friendly service" only to encounter a grouchy receptionist who answered the phone. Yikes. Guess someone forgot to give her the memo. And whether you think it fair or not, that is a direct reflection on *your business as a whole*. That is another book to write, but hire carefully and train them well!

How do you go beyond mere puffery and prove your case that you are friendlier, more valuable, offer better service and are more dependable than every other option they have available?

Allow me to share with you one straightforward way to do this that will drastically differentiate you from every competitor, both directly and indirectly. As a bonus, it is very simple to do; it is extremely cost effective and when compiled, can be used in a variety of different outlets and mediums. What I am referring to is customer testimonials.

Testify! The Selling Power of Customer Testimonials

If you want to increase your closing rates without resorting to fancy tricks or learning a quagmire of new skills, just become an avid collector of testimonials. I don't care what anyone else says, they work.

Consider this: If I told you I was the greatest business mentor and marketing consultant of all time, would you believe me? Probably not. But what if your friend called and told you I was the greatest mentor and marketing consultant of all time? Then you *might* move a little closer to believing it.

But, what if your lawyer, your doctor, your mother, your children's principal, the head of your trade association and the guy you buy tomatoes from at the local farmer's market told you I was the greatest business mentor and marketing consultant of all time?

I bet you would be *much* more interested in sitting down and having a talk with me then, would you not? You would probably think a great deal more of my capabilities after hearing of them out in the community rather than from me bragging about my skills.

This is such a simple principle that it makes me wonder why *all* businesses don't use testimonials. I really don't know why. Personally, I think it should be a requirement of doing business. When it comes to raising your closing and sales rates, a good series of testimonials can make all the difference.

Now let me show you when, where and how to get these top-notch testimonials that will increase the believability of your offers and services.

How to Become an Avid Collector of Testimonials

If you go searching for opportunities to get testimonials, you will find it is relatively easy and in no time you will begin to collect them.

The best opportunity is when your customer is "in heat," meaning striking while the transaction iron is hot and they are madly in love with you. Let's say you have just done something that wowed them. They might come in to pay their bill and say "I can't believe what a wonderful service you provided my family. It was much better than the last five companies I've gone to!"

This is your chance! You say, "Thank you! Would it be okay if I shared your story with others who might be interested in our services as well? It really helps us better serve our clients!"

Or, you can say, "Thank you! Would it be okay if I wrote down what you just said and shared it with others? It would mean a lot to me!" Then just write down (or, better yet, have them write it down) what was said and have them approve it by signing it.

Another option, simply say: "Thank you! Did you know that one of the best ways we get good clients like you is by sharing the success stories of our past clients? Would it be okay if we quoted you in some of our marketing and sales communications?"

It is wise to ask them if you can share their name, or first name with last initial, just to be on the safe side. At least determine their preference; never assume anything. Again, it is always best to have them write down their testimonial or record it with their expressed permission.

Do not make this harder than it has to be. KISS, remember? Keep your marketing strategies simple. The main key is to get them when they are in a good mood. Ask if you can have their permission to quote them and share their story. Then get their testimonial. That's it. Keep it simple.

If you do nothing else, collect testimonials from customers who are in heat and have just expressed how appreciative they are of you and your services.

Another appropriate time to collect a testimonial is when you somehow *save the day*. Did you do something for a customer that was out of the ordinary? Maybe you made an emergency house call at 8:30 at night to fix a small leak, free of charge. Or perhaps they wanted something that was supposedly discontinued, but you went the extra mile and tracked down what they were looking for (even if it were with one of your competitors).

Anytime you save the day, just ask them for a testimonial. Do it. In fact, I intentionally look for opportunities to save the day, because it serves in the best interest of my business. If I go the extra mile, then I know they will give me a great testimonial! Once again, this is the best word of mouth marketing you can get.

Once you get good at the first two, consider putting out a customer survey once in a while. Postcard surveys are inexpensive and quick. If you run a restaurant, this can be done easily at the table or counter. Other businesses may need to send them by mail. Offer an incentive if they return the survey promptly.

To glean testimonials out of this, have the customer answer a few key questions. Then, retype those answers in a letter format, and ask them to sign off on it as a testimonial that you can share with others, with their permission, of course.

There are more aggressive ways to get testimonials, and I would encourage you to be aggressive about getting them, especially after you have gotten the knack for getting the low hanging fruit. Once you get used to asking your "hot" customers and those for whom you've saved the day, experiment with actively seeking out testimonials to further prove your case.

How to Use the Testimonial for Maximum Effect

I am going to share some examples that you can literally knock off and use in your own business. You can also use them for brainstorming purposes on your own ideas.

Let's return to the phone book advertising example. Instead of the typical puffery, your ad might include something that says in effect: "Look, any business can say that they care about the customer and that they are dependable and have high quality service. Instead of us tooting our own horn, maybe you would rather hear it from some of our customers themselves. Just call our satisfied customer hotline to hear a pre-recorded message of what some of our customers think about our services."

Do you know how much a voice mail account costs? About four dollars per month. For that measly amount you can create a recording of your best customers.

How do you get these recordings? Perhaps you have one of your sales reps call your customers a few days after the sale. Explain to the customer that for quality issues, would it be okay if you recorded the call? This can be done inexpensively with a digital phone recorder that costs less than fifty bucks or through an online service for about ten dollars a month.

Ask them what their thoughts were on the service or for the product. At the end, ask them if it would be okay if you shared their thoughts with other customers who might be interested in the products or services. You might offer the customer another incentive for this. That is just one way to get your testimonials recorded. There are others.

Now you have a tool. You have people talking about how good you are. You can put this prerecorded message into your various marketing communications! Your believability goes through the roof.

Another thing to consider is compiling a booklet of your best testimonials. Do you know any other business that has a testimonial booklet? Would you think that distinguishes you from your competitors? I guarantee it does—and in an effective way!

Let's say you really went the extra mile and totally knock it out of the park for a customer. They were so happy they called you to thank you personally for the great service. They were so impressed with you because you went above and beyond the call of duty.

This is a golden opportunity to ask them if it would be okay to feature them as case study in your next advertisement. Then you could write an advertisement that really looks like an article (or an article for your newsletter), where you simply tell the story of what you did for this customer and their glorious response.

This type of advertisement is about a million times more effective than the ads that scream at you to "BUY MY PRODUCT!" At the very least, you should include some testimonials in your advertising, just to enhance your claims.

Anatomy of a Good Testimonial

Now, some people have half-assed tried some sort of a testimonial system and told me that they don't work. That reminds me of my mom telling me several years ago that her DVD player didn't work. I asked, "Did you plug it in?"

Oops. No.

So, there's that.

Testimonials are like anything else—if you do them poorly they probably will not work. To do them right, you must know what a good testimonial looks like.

Here is a not-so-great testimonial: "You did a good job."

Here's a great testimonial:

> "You responded to our call and made it to our house in less than thirty minutes. The last company we called took two hours to get there. Not only that, you helped us save over thirteen percent of the original cost. Thank you so much!"

> Dave and Lisa B., novelty bookstore owners, Ashville, NC

The difference is obvious. Bad testimonials are bland and really don't say anything of specific value. Good testimonials are specific and give hard facts. I love it when someone says to me, "I read your book on Saturday and did one new thing I learned that resulted in me making $772.18 in profit by the following Friday. You're a genius!"

That is a far better testimonial than, "Your suggestions helped my business a lot." Blah.

Not only are specifics needed, but it is good to have a name, location and occupation. Otherwise people will think that maybe you are just making up the testimonials yourself, even though that is definitely a deceptive practice (which is why audio and video testimonials with permission are the best). You do not want that.

There are other things that can influence your testimonials. Humans are hardwired by nature to trust authority. That is why testimonials from experts such as scientists, doctors, professors, fire fighters, and other esteemed positions tend to have more social pull than regular testimonials. Just think how credible a testimonial must be in relation to the product or services you are selling.

So, set a plan in action. Come up with the different ways you are going to capture and use testimonials, and make sure everybody in your business starts to become a testimonial collector. It really is one of the easiest ways to increase your sales closing percentage—and it's great for business which gives you more reason to celebrate!

WORKBOOK – CHAPTER 5

Describe three techniques you will use to get testimonials in your particular business scenario. Train your staff as well.

1.

2.

3.

Have someone begin to create a testimonial booklet or consider adding new customer testimonials to your newsletter or ezine. List your possibilities here as you begin to organize your special offers.

Chapter Six

THE WIDE, WIDE WORLD OF VARIETY MARKETING

In *The KISS System: Stress-Free Marketing Strategies to Boost Your Local Business on a Budget* we have mainly selected to discuss how to address your 'grassroots' clients. Grassroots marketing is the principle of targeting and grooming a select group of your clients to encourage them to spread your message organically by word of mouth. This is where social media can accentuate your efforts.

Targeted marketing campaigns geared specifically to your existing customer base is cost effective. If you have a limited advertising budget, spend what you do have to attract those who already know, like and trust you. They are the key to bringing in new business and turning those individuals into your next level of loyal customers.

If You *Must* Place Printed Ads...

Have you noticed that most print ads look the same? We discussed this earlier. There is a problem with going with the norm—you risk getting normal results, if any.

With your business and livelihood on the line, I hope you are not content with ordinary results, especially when extraordinary results are so easy to obtain, even with newspaper or other printed advertising. You only need to do a few simple things differently.

The first thing to understand is what people are looking for when they open the newspaper or ad section. Some people are looking for specific contact information. If they already have a specific service provider in mind, it is going to be hard to woo those people over (not saying it can't be done). But the good news is when most people open the phonebook and go to the Yellow Pages, for instance, they are looking for information to help them find the best business to contact that will give them the solution they desire.

Consumers want...

- a good deal

- to do business with someone who understands their needs and leads them to the best solution at an affordable rate

- to deal with as little headaches, delays and customer service problems as possible

Now, flip open to the ads section in your phone book and see if any of the advertisements address the above criteria. You will most likely find that hardly any of them do the job adequately. Good. That will make it much easier for you.

I am going to show you how to create a simple print ad that will make people believe that if they contact you or go into your store that they are going to get the best solution for their dollars. Let them know it will be easy and convenient to deal with you and that you are the best choice for their options.

If you can pull that off, then you are going to get the lion's share of customers that used to search in the back of the phonebook or in newspapers for help in your industry.

Use the following techniques in all of your media properties; all of your written content—your websites, newsletters, on all social media and any local print ads you may create.

The Most Important Part of Your Ad

The world's best ad is no better than the world's worst ad if no one sees it. The first job a printed ad (or any ad, for that matter) must do is grab the attention of the people who are best matched to take advantage of the services and products that you offer.

The easiest way to do that is with a good attention-getting **headline**. To understand what a good headline looks like, let's first look at some bad ones. I sorted through my own local Yellow Pages, and found these headlines:

"The Blind Factory"

"Cyclists Serving Cyclists"

"Wet Basement or Crawl Space"

"Quality Construction"

"Professional Muffler, Inc."

"Old Fashioned Values, Including Our Own People Doing the Work"

These are all terrible headlines, in my humble opinion. Almost all of them talk about the service provider and not the person who is seeking specific services. Talk about self-centered! Typical for today, huh? No. You must be different. Advertisements are supposed to be all about the *customer* and *their* needs, remember?

None of the ads above promise any benefit to the customer; none of them get the person reading excited about their services, and most are nothing more than the name of the company. The customer must be able to say, "There! That's the one for me!" when they see the right ad.

Finally, respect your headline. It is the most important part of your ad so you need to do better than the rest. Ideally, you want a headline that promises a *benefit to the reader*, and is written to grab the attention of a certain large segment of the population who is best matched for the goods and services you provide.

Let's take a look at the first one: The Blind Factory. How could this one be improved? Here is a good headline that I have found to get great results: "The Five Mistakes Most People Make When They Purchase Blinds for Their Home." Or, "Warning: Don't Buy Blinds Until You Read This." Or even, "How to Get the Best Blinds for Your Home in 48 Hours or Less, Guaranteed!"

Notice the difference with these headlines?
- First, it's important to note that they focus on the *consumer* and their particular *needs*.
- Second, they promise a huge *benefit*.
- Third, they call out a *certain segment* of the general population. In this case they are addressing people who are looking to purchase blinds, who want to get a good deal, want ease of service, or want to make sure they don't commit a mistake when buying blinds.

Once you have a good headline, the ad practically writes itself. For example, let's return to the headline: "The Five Mistakes People Make When They Purchase Blinds for Their Home." You would then identify the five mistakes that you find people tend to make if they don't have an expert to help them select their product. Then, after you introduce each mistake, explain how that mistake can be avoided if they come into your store.

Remember, people who turn to the ad sections are generally looking for information to help them make the right decision on finding the best service provider. Typically, the person who provides the most information wins—and it helps if that information is beneficial to the reader and strictly focused on their immediate needs.

If you do a quick review of a typical printed ad, you will note that it has fifty words or less and is usually filled with puffery. For example, I always see this: "The customer comes first." I say talk to the hand or prove it! Walk the talk. Like my grandfather always used to tell me, "Say what you mean, mean what you say." That's some sage advice.

This leads us to the second biggest point about writing effective printed ads: Making powerful, unique claims to demonstrate that you provide the services better than any other solution that is available.

How can you make a unique claim that demonstrates that the customer truly comes first? Here is a technique that has been used to great effect. The first thing on the list is to contact some of your past satisfied customers. Ask them to write a quick one paragraph testimonial about what they liked most about dealing with your company. It is easy to do this with the strategies we have discussed.

Then, put those testimonials on your website and social media, such as on your Facebook page. In your ad you could say, "You can read what seventy-two satisfied customers had to say about our great products at www.(what-ever-your-site).com" and invite traffic to your website in this manner.

People looking at the ad may not visit your website, but it will have the effect of demonstrating to them that not only does the customer truly come first, but you have seventy-two of your own customers who claim that you *do* put them first. Yours will be the only ad in your category that can claim that, so in a potential customer's mind you would be the preferred source if customer service is their main priority.

Your ad should contain at least one dramatic example of proof to validate your claims. It is best if you have specific numbers or facts to verify it and testimonials to back it up. These are powerful ways of demonstrating that you offer great service and goods, and that you follow through on your end of the bargain.

For example, you can do much better than merely stating

something like "In business since 1994!" My first reaction when I see this statement is "What does that mean for me and my immediate needs?"

The fact is I know several bad companies that have somehow managed to stay shakily in business for decades. Instead, you can say "We have successfully helped over 10,417 clients in Englewood find just the right blinds for their home."

So, first come up with a powerful headline. Then expand on that headline in your ad. Also remember to throw in at least one dramatic example of proof to validate your claims.

Another thing to note and avoid. Surprisingly, I often see an ad placed for a business or organization, but I cannot find an address or phone number on the ad space. The ad is essentially your billboard. Make sure the information is there without having to get eye strain trying to find it—make it clear as day. KISS, remember?

Now you're ready for the finale: The **offer** and the **call to action**.

How to Create an Offer and a Call to Action

Every single ad, regardless of the media in which it appears, must have an offer and a call-to-action to accept that offer in order to be even remotely effective. A call to action means that you tell the customer exactly what they need to do immediately after reading the ad to take advantage of it.

People are motivated to take action based on emotion. They look for solutions to address their fear, their pain, their problem. The more you can offer them solutions, they more excited they get and the more they see the potential for the results they seek.

Let me start with the best call to action, although it is also the most complicated one to set up. You ideally want to establish a continuing relationship with people who are interested in doing business with you, so if they are initially hesitant, further communication can get them in the door.

The best way to do that is to offer something free to the user if they contact you. Here's a simple way of doing that. Let's go back to the window blinds example.

The first thing you should do is to write a focused report on "How to Pick the Most Beautiful Blinds for Your Home on a Shoestring Budget" (or something to that effect). You could add this article to your newsletter. Your marketing consultant can also help you with any copywriting services you need. Using the valuable information contained in the report, offer the customer the best tips for getting the most value from their purchase.

Save the report in PDF format so that it can be used in an email that you can send to your customers later if you choose. This allows you to have people sign up for an email list and you can send them email offers in the future.

Steps to Crafting a Simplified Irresistible Offer

When people sign up for your email list, they will automatically receive your free digital report on "How to Pick the Most Beautiful Blinds for Your Home on a Shoestring Budget." Not only that, you can use an email auto-responder to send a few follow up messages automatically at certain intervals to anyone who signs up.

In your ads you say, "If you would like to receive our free report on "How to Pick the Most Beautiful Blinds for Your Home on a Shoestring Budget" visit our website at www.(what-ever-your-site).com." This drives your customers to a page that explains that to get the report they just have to enter in their name and email into the form (and other identifying information you choose).

Of course, in the report you will list your contact information so the potential customer can easily contact you and become your regular customer.

This is by far the best strategy but also the most complex. A simple strategy is to make a "This Ad Only" offer. In this case you say, "If you call today and schedule an appointment, mention this particular ad and we will give you a special discounted 20% off any one item. Offer good today only." In any case, you are *enticing* them to respond to your ad. If they do all the things in this report, then you are going to have an ad that is dramatically different than everyone else's which will allow you to get dramatically better results!

In essence, your offer should:

- ✓ Explain the special deal they are getting and its value

- ✓ Include testimonials from satisfied customers

- ✓ Offer a limited supply (create scarcity)

- ✓ Include the Call to Action such as: Click Here, Sign Up Now

Location, Location, Location

Do you have a website? Please say you have a website. A dedicated Facebook page can often serve the same purpose. There are also other internet sites such as Instagram and Pinterest that can highlight your business well. I like to call websites and social media accounts "media properties." After all, it is very much like owning real estate. You own that corner of the world wide web. Make the most of it.

Local online directories vastly help the consumer find about anything they are looking for on the web. Local search engines like Google, Yahoo, MSN/Bing have been a gamechanger for the success of local businesses. Social media marketing, blogging, videos, and lead capture are among the top ways of ranking higher for your keywords thus attracting more clients. Word of advice: Google your own business, then "claim" it when prompted. As of this writing, Google sends you a postcard in the mail to complete the verification process, but it is well worth it. There is an app called Google My Business. Download that and follow the prompts.

Five Proven Internet Strategies to Explode Your Local Sales

Did you know that here are over one billion local internet searches done every month? One *billion*—and growing! Eighty percent of individuals searching for a specific product or service will do an internet search first, before making a purchase from newspaper ads or the ever-increasingly obsolete phone book.

There are some important components in creating a good online marketing strategy that you need to know about. You want to show up in multiple areas online; do not just rely on one area. Setting your business up online properly now will help you cash in on the early gold rush and crush your competitors. Here are the five categories upon which to focus for your online marketing campaigns.

#1: Social Media Marketing

A little blue birdie recently told me that if you aren't tweeting you may be cheating yourself out of a huge opportunity in your marketing strategies for your business. Twitter has seen a rise in popularity in recent years. Its popularity along with Facebook and blogs (web logs) has forced the issue and it is time to take notice. A savvy business marketer will take full advantage of these media types. Instagram and Pinterest are fast becoming great avenues for product sales. LinkedIn is a social networking site that targets professionals and offers networking opportunities between past and present colleagues as well as business to business communication.

Social media is any media that uses a web-based technology to facilitate social interaction. It appears that we are quickly evolving from a digital world where information was the marketable commodity to a communications market where new methods of socializing and networking are constantly being introduced. Blogs, wikis, RSS newsfeeds, podcasts, video socialization built around applications like Facebook, Twitter and YouTube are recently formulated methods of communication that seemingly overnight have developed with literally hundreds of millions, if not billions, of active participants.

With several types of social media literally at your fingertips, you have access to a low cost, highly effective means of spreading your message to a relatively large audience, for fun or for business. Use the Messenger app in Facebook to communicate in real time with your customers. According to Facebook's research, fifty-three percent of consumers are more likely to shop with a company they can message directly.

With over two billion (and counting) active members, Facebook is a giant that will not be ignored—and it isn't going away any time soon. Social networks have changed the way people research and make their buying decisions. The advertising opportunities are truly astronomical! You have the capability to create laser targeted ads tweaked down to the age, birthdate, likes and dislikes of your customers. And that's only the tip of the iceberg. Visit www.thekissmarketingsystem.com for a free download report on Facebook advertising.

This being said, you still need to identify methods that are most appropriate for your specific target audience and business entity, as well as your budget. Remember, go where they go. This is another opportunity to use a focus group of customers.

When a solid internet presence is leveraged properly in your favor you will have the opportunity to build more trust, respect, and credibility with your customers than ever before.

Imagine being able to have feedback on how to improve your business and sell more on a daily basis. Imagine being able to turn every customer into a potential raving fan that will "Like" you and will advertise for you. As mentioned earlier, putting it all together can be a bit daunting. There are many tutorials that will walk you through setting up social media marketing campaigns. But a good marketing professional can make that happen, too. Thanks to the internet I am exclusively available to my clients no matter where they are—or wherever I may roam!).

Your social media accounts garner you almost immediate contact with your friends and followers. Watch for social trends then set up campaigns accordingly to capitalize on them in the heat of the moment.

#2: Local Internet Search, Presence, and Visibility

Did you know that eighty-five percent of all searches online now include a city or local term (for example: Pineville Plumbers)? This number is up from the thirty percent only a few years ago! Local consumers are searching for local services—period.

This means that every search term will have area businesses figuring out how to get listed in all of the local directories. The search engine aspect of the internet can be quite daunting. You must utilize the most powerful and targeted keywords that pertain to your business, services or products but this climate is changing. Again, claim your business on each of the search engine sites and visit the Google Keyword Planner to get targeted keywords and phrases that you need to use in all of your written content. Everywhere you spread your word.

Claiming your business online gives you the opportunity to add pictures, menu items, and so much more that you can offer your customer immediately.

It goes without saying that your customers cannot hire you if they cannot find you. Once again, you can do this, but your marketer can also help make sure that your local business is found on Google, Bing, Yahoo and other search engines when a potential customer types in appropriate keywords that fit your business. This affects how you rank so that your neighbors can easily find you online.

If you are well versed in all things internet, you may be able to tackle this one yourself. I have to say that sometimes it is best to concentrate on running your business successfully and let your marketing professional handle the more complicated strategies of internet advertising. It is easy to lose valuable time and a lot of money if you are not well-versed in this type of media advertising. Know your limits.

Here's a slick trick to implement for your business. Go to **http://geositemapgenerator.com** and enter your business information. This adds what is called a geotag to your business and increases your standings in searchability. I will also take this opportunity to remind you about an app called Google My Business. Download the app and follow the easy prompts to set it up. Again, you will be mailed a postcard with a verification code in order to complete the process. Make sure you check it frequently to keep your information up to date. Your customers appreciate that.

#3: Internet Lead Capture and Follow-Ups

Did you know that even a great webpage will only convert, at best, five percent of its visitors to make a purchase? It is absolutely true. This means that nineteen out of twenty visitors to your website are destined to surf away into the ether world and could stumble across your competitor's website instead.

However, the average page that offers consumers free information in exchange for their contact info gets a much higher conversion rate, up to thirty-five to forty percent. That is significantly more substantial, which validates the importance of your offer of a free written report, a coupon, a discount, a checklist or some other item of value.

The consumer visits your site; you offer a free report or an eBook; *they must enter their name and email address* (more if you so require) to receive it, and voila! You have the beginnings of your email list of customers. There are other ways to obtain email addresses. The brief survey card we discussed earlier is another method.

Imagine being able to instantly increase your return on leads seven-fold and do it with push button automation. This is possible. If you know your way around the computer, you could easily set these up yourself. Otherwise, a good computer savvy marketing professional can help you do just that. Once it has been set up, it is really pretty uncomplicated to maintain it yourself or use a designee.

This is a great way to capture leads as discussed previously. Engage your marketing consultant or a copywriter for assistance if writing isn't your thing. After all, your time and talents are best used running a successful business.

#4: Video Marketing

Would you believe that there are over twenty-six *billion* videos viewed per month in the United States alone? What's more, YouTube is the fourth highest rated search engine on the internet, which means that right this minute somebody could be searching for your services online in the form of a video. Will they find you?

Imagine if you had the advertising budget to run infomercials twenty-four hours a day, seven days a week—you would dominate your market! That's the power of video marketing. This is possible on a shoestring (even in a rough economy) and you can create more trust and respect with your customers than ever before.

A marketing video can be in the form of a simple cell phone snippets, a Power Point presentation or full-blown videography. Since more and more people are turning to the internet to quickly search for information, the use of video is an effective means of capturing the customer's attention by delivering the information quickly and easily.

By using video in your marketing and advertising campaigns, you can demonstrate the proper use of a one of your products or services in a virtual setting. Just remember that the search engines are attracted to videos, so prepare for more traffic to your site. Keep your videos short, sweet, and to the point to avoid boredom and the eventual fleeing of the viewer. Two minutes run-time is a good rule of thumb for an online video to keep the adult attention span tuned to your station.

You can demonstrate virtually anything on YouTube. Pet grooming, a new recipe, how to install just-about-anything! Remember that the purpose of a video is to promote your business, to capture views of potential customers and, hopefully, turn them into sales and finally, a loyal customer.

#5: Blogging

It is estimated that seventy-seven percent of all internet users follow one or more blogs (web log). If you are not capitalizing on this growing community, you are missing out on targeted advertising opportunities to reach more of the masses.

A blog is often a blend between what is occurring on the web, in the marketplace, or in one's life. Bloggers, sometimes also called Infopreneurs these days, are passionate about sharing what they love, and if you have one as a client and can turn them into a raving Fan, they can propel your business to new heights.

A blog is very easy to set up and maintain. It is a wonderful way to open the conversation with potential customers and gain valuable insights to buying habits.

You can join a blog already in progress or start your own. Wordpress.com, Blogger.com and Blog.com are among the most used blogs though there are many others that are free and fairly user friendly. Share your site liberally wherever your footsteps take you, online or off!

Blogs are useful for the sake of business in that you can obtain customer leads through them as well as place affiliate ads and links on your page which means you earn a commission if a product is sold from your site. But blogs are great for personal use, too. You can practice your writing or encourage thought provoking conversations, whatever. You name it.

It's your blog…do what you want to do! And you will be surprised at how many other people visit your little corner of the World Wide Web.

A recent study quoted that sixty percent of marketers say that blog content creation is their top inbound marketing focus. And more than eighty percent of businesses surveyed said that their company blog was "useful to critical" for their business. That should give you pause. Visit the sites I listed above and get started.

Invite your customers to contribute articles to your blog or ezine (electronic magazine). Highlight a customer appreciation program. Or again, this is another inexpensive opportunity to engage a high school or college student if you don't feel confident in your skills or simply don't have the time or interest in writing.

Hint: Always allow someone else be your proofreader. Another set of eyes helps find errors before you hit the 'publish' key and can apply the polishing touch.

WORKBOOK – CHAPTER 6

PRINT ADS CHECKLIST:

- ☐ Attention-grabbing headline

- ☐ Focused solely on the consumer and their needs and desires

- ☐ Promise a significant benefit to the reader

- ☐ Call out a section of the general population – your niche

- ☐ Make a powerful, unique or bold, but truthful, claim stating that your services are better than those of any other solution available

- ☐ Make sure your contact information is in clear sight; address, phone number, email, etc.

SOCIAL MEDIA CHECKLIST: write your user name for each.

- ☐ Facebook

- ☐ Twitter

- ☐ YouTube / Vimeo

- ☐ Instagram

- ☐ Pinterest

- ☐ LinkedIn

- ☐ Google My Business

Conclusion

In conclusion, don't drag your feet or self yourself short, like I did in the beginning. The goal of laser-targeted marketing strategies is obviously to increase your bottom line profits year after year. I hope you afford yourself every opportunity to lose the 'thinking box' where your competitors are still spinning their wheels in frustration.

Get in step with today's competitive, sometimes complicated, local marketing environment. You *can* easily out-do your competitors! Use every advantage I have given you in this book to create your own work of *art*—your creative marketing masterpiece. Seriously, get engaged with your loyal customers through effective marketing strategies. This pays off.

To accent your marketing endeavors, look for the right marketing professional best suited to assist you and your unique business needs if you need. They must listen to you intently, exude creativity and be well-versed in today's complicated marketing strategies. I am not saying it can't be done to go it on your own, but it can be extremely daunting for a business owner or manager to handle advertising when your time and talents are better used for running your business.

The internet has indeed made the globe shrink in the virtual sense. You have immediate access to, and can communicate with, individuals in every time zone around the planet at any given moment in time.

Take advantage of mobile marketing and Internet searching techniques, first and foremost. Your customers are virtually at your fingertips! Send out a text or an app blast or a Facebook post when business is slow. Maybe there was an appointment cancellation that can be refilled by another client waiting anxiously to take their place. Let them know about it!

The restaurant crowds can catch the busy family rush and students during the mid-week, or the football fanatics on Sunday afternoons by offering specials to get them in the door. To add to the fun and frolic on game day (or during a political election), you can arrange to sponsor Facebook or cell phone surveys or voting polls among your clientele. The possibilities are endless.

In today's economy and tough competitive marketplace, your customers will acknowledge your added attention to detail for them. They appreciate and count on exclusive offers and coupons from their favorite businesses. They *want* to give you their commerce and loyalty.

Hone your art of advertising your piece of commerce. By making it worth their while, customers enjoy the discounts they receive, and you get the additional business you need. No matter how you chalk it up, that's a win-win!

If you find yourself becoming overwhelmed, you only have to remember one thing. Remember the KISS System. Keep It Simple, Stupid.

And—it isn't stupid if it works.

About the Author

Author, speaker and mentor **Connie Gorrell** is passionate about helping entrepreneurs in all walks of life identify and establish their personal and professional goals, especially while overcoming adversity. Her personal goal to *pay it forward* comes through her authentic wisdom and experience which resonates with those who struggle to find their way to overcome obstacles in life. She established a nationally based business offering continuing education credits for healthcare professionals before life threw her family a series of tragedies with the deaths of her children. As a result, Connie comes from a place of deep humility with the passion to help other business owners succeed in their local marketplace regardless of life's cruel curveballs.

Connie and her husband Brent are the founders and directors of The DreamSTRONG™ Foundation. She is president of Barefoot Execs., Inc., an independent lifestyle brand educator and publisher. As an entrepreneur and businesswoman, Connie knows the importance of strategic planning based on individual needs and market analysis.

Connie's philosophy is to under-promise and over-deliver when it comes to customer satisfaction and teaches various methods in her workshops. She stresses the fact that businesses are easily located on the internet and cautions her clients to take necessary steps to never run out of leads. The goal is to transform potential clients into lifetime customers and raving "fans" that "Like" them loyally.

Connie enjoys hearing from her readers. If you have concerns about how to improve your business' bottom line or questions regarding any of the strategies listed in this book, please refer to contact information below.

Connect with Connie!
www.conniegorrell.com
www.facebook.com/conniegorrell
www.twitter.com/conniegorrell
www.linkedin.com/in/conniegorrell
www.instagram.com/conniegorrell

Enjoy some of Connie's other books, too!
All Available on Amazon

The Gift of Inspiration for Women

*An enchanting daybook, sure to be your true companion. **100% of all proceeds** go directly to support the DreamSTRONG Foundation scholarship program for women and girls.*

Postcards From Paradise

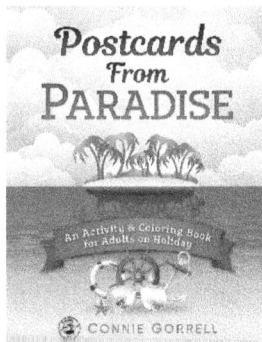

A fun activity book for adults on vacation. Enjoy coloring pages, puzzles and journal pages, too. Perfect book to help you relax and enjoy the holiday, even if you vacation at home!

The Invisible Thread: True Stories of Synchronicity

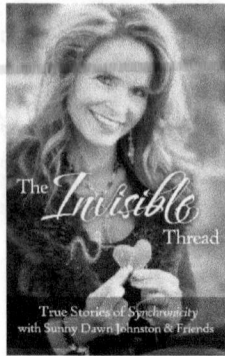

Published and contributed by Connie Gorrell.
Featuring Sunny Dawn Johnston.

How to Brand YOU! A Quick Step-By-Step Guide to Personal & Professional Branding

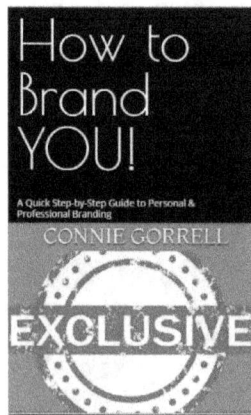

Available in Kindle only!

Take a stress break and do something fun!

Successfully navigate your way through the local marketplace.

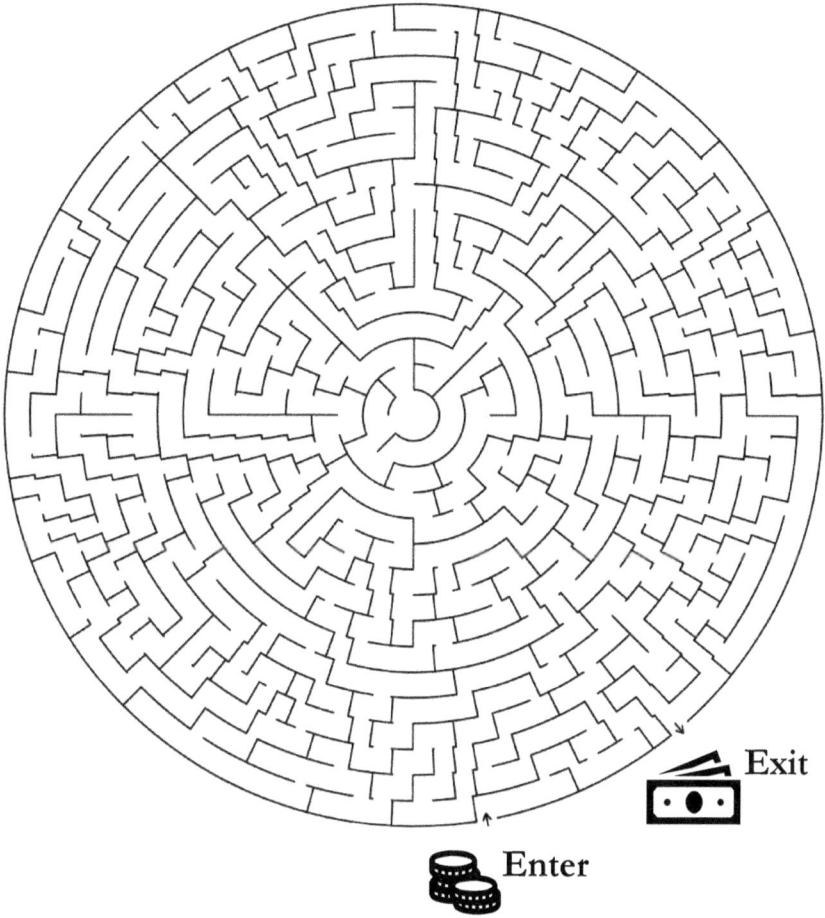

Exit

Enter

Puzzle Solution

There is always a solution to your marketing needs.

Visit www.thekissmarketingsystem.com for more resources!

Legal Disclaimer

This book is strictly for informational purposes. The author and/or publisher does not guarantee that following these techniques, suggestions, tips, ideas, or strategies will be successful for the reader. This book contains business strategies and marketing methods that, regardless of the author's personal results and experience, may not produce the same results for the reader. We make no guarantee, expressed or implied, that by following the strategies within, you will make money or increase current profits or customer base, as there are several factors and variables that come into play regarding any given business model. Results will depend on the nature of the product, service or business, the conditions of the marketplace, the experience of the individual, and other elements beyond common control. This book is for general purposes only and the reader is encouraged to use only those techniques that directly apply to their business type. It is the reader's responsibility to conduct due diligence regarding the safe and successful operation of their particular business.